ADOBE® DREAMWEAVER® CS3

CLASSROOM IN A BOOK®

The official training workbook from Adobe Systems

Adobe

Adobe Press books are published by Peachpit, Berkeley, CA. To report errors, please send a note to errata@peachpit.com.

Printed in the U.S.A.

ISBN-13: 978-0-321-49981-3
ISBN-10:   0-321-49981-6

9 8 7 6 5 4 3 2

Contents

Getting Started

About Classroom in a Book. 1

Prerequisites 1

Installing the program 2

Copying the Classroom in a Book files. 2

Setting Preferences 3

Additional resources. 3

Adobe Certification 4

1   Quick Start to Dreamweaver CS3

Selecting a CSS starting point 8

Saving your page. 9

Modifying the page title 10

Changing headings. 10

Inserting text. 11

Adding new images 12

Linking to other pages. 14

Selecting and modifying CSS styles 15

Previewing your page in a browser 22

Review questions. 26

Review answers 26

2   Customizing your Workspace

Touring the workspace. 29

Creating custom workspaces 45

Using the Property inspector 46

Adjusting toolbars. 49

Personalizing Preferences 54

Review questions. 56

Review answers 56

3 **Applying Cascading Style Sheets**

Defining a Dreamweaver site 59

Previewing your completed file. 61

Attaching an external style sheet 62

Creating new CSS rules 65

Applying styles. 70

Changing properties. 72

Developing a Print style sheet 73

Review questions. 80

Review answers 80

4 **Working with Text**

Previewing your completed file. 83

Entering headlines and body text. 84

Importing external text 87

Creating numbered and bulleted lists. 90

Spell checking your document 92

Searching and replacing text 94

Building tables 96

Importing tabular data. 100

Review questions. 103

Review answers 103

5 **Designing with Images**

Previewing your completed file. 105

Inserting an image 106

Using background images 110

Optimizing graphics 112

Including Fireworks rollovers 117

Inserting Photoshop files 121

Copying and pasting from Photoshop 124

Accessing Bridge 126

Review questions. 129

Review answers 129

6   Inserting Links

Previewing your completed file. 133

Linking to internal site pages. 134

Creating an external link 137

Setting up email links. 138

Targeting links within the page. 139

Review questions. 143

Review answers 143

7   Crafting Page Layouts

Previewing your completed file. 145

Creating layout styled div elements. 146

Exporting CSS styles 168

Using the Ruler and Guides 170

Review questions. 174

Review answers 174

8   Creating Interactive Pages

Learning about Dreamweaver Behaviors 177

Previewing your completed file. 180

Applying behaviors. 182

Opening browser windows. 187

Modifying a behavior 189

Showing and hiding areas. 192

Review questions. 198

Review answers 198

9   Integrating Ajax with Spry

Learning about Ajax and Spry 201

Previewing your completed file. 203

Including XML data. 205

Building Spry data sets. 210

Applying Spry Detail Regions. 213

Constructing Spry Widgets. 216

Applying Spry Effects 222

Review questions. 225

Review answers 225

10 Constructing Forms

Previewing your completed file. 229

Learning about forms. 232

Adding a form to the page 233

Inserting text form elements 235

Including radio buttons 247

Inserting checkboxes 250

Working with lists 253

Adding a submit button to a form 256

Styling your forms 257

Review questions. 262

Review answers 262

11 Adding Multimedia

Previewing your completed file. 265

Placing a Flash movie on the Web 267

Showing Flash video. 271

Integrating a Flash slide show 274

Review questions. 282

Review answers 282

12 Publishing to the Web

Defining a remote site 285

Validating your site 297

Putting your site online 299

Review questions. 302

Review answers 302

What's on the CD*

Here is an overview of the contents of the Classroom in a Book CD

Lesson files . . . and so much more

The *Adobe Dreamweaver CS3 Classroom in a Book* CD includes the lesson files that you'll need to complete the exercises in this book, as well as other content to help you learn more about Adobe Dreamweaver and use it with greater efficiency and ease. The diagram below represents the contents of the CD, which should help you locate the files you need.

Lessons

Each lesson has its own folder inside the Lessons folder. You will need to copy these lesson folders to your hard drive before you can begin each lesson.

Videos

A sampling of QuickTime** tutorial movies from lynda.com are located in the Movies folder as well as information about other video training products offered by lynda.com.

Adobe Design Center

Go to www.adobe.com/designcenter/ <http://www.adobe.com/designcenter/> to find tutorials, ideas from design experts, and thought provoking articles on how today's designer's engage with technology and what that means for design, design tools, and society.

** *The latest version of Apple QuickTime can be downloaded from www.apple.com/quicktime/download.*

Getting Started

Adobe® Dreamweaver® CS3 is the industry-leading Web authoring program. Whether you create websites for a living or one for your own business, Dreamweaver offers you all the tools you need to get professional quality results.

About Classroom in a Book

Adobe Dreamweaver CS3 Classroom in a Book® is part of the official training series for Adobe graphics and publishing software from Adobe Systems, Inc.

The lessons are designed so that you can learn at your own pace. If you're new to Adobe Dreamweaver, you'll learn the fundamentals you need to put the program to work. If you are an experienced user, you'll find that Classroom in a Book teaches many advanced features, including tips and techniques for using the latest version of Adobe Dreamweaver.

Although each lesson provides step-by-step instructions for creating a specific project, there's room for exploration and experimentation. You can follow the book from start to finish or do only the lessons that correspond to your interests and needs. Each lesson concludes with a review section summarizing what you've covered.

Prerequisites

Before beginning to use Adobe Dreamweaver CS3 Classroom in a Book, you should have a working knowledge of your computer and its operating system. Make sure you know how to use the mouse and standard menus and commands, and also how to open, save, and close files. If you need to review these techniques, see the printed or online documentation included with your Windows or Mac OS documentation.

Note: When instructions differ by platform, Windows commands appear first, and then the Mac OS command, with the platform noted in parentheses. For example, "press Alt (Windows) or Option (MacOS) and click away from the graphic."

Installing the program

Before you begin using Adobe Dreamweaver CS3 Classroom in a Book, make sure that your system is set up correctly and that you've installed the required software and hardware.

You must purchase the Adobe Dreamweaver CS3 software separately. For complete instructions on installing the software, see the "How to Install" Readme file on the application CD.

Copying the Classroom in a Book files

The Classroom in a Book CD includes folders containing all the electronic files for the lessons. Each lesson has its own folder. You must install these folders on your hard disk to use the files for the lessons. To save room on your hard disk, you can install the folders for each lesson as you need them. It is strongly recommended that all lesson folders are stored within a single folder on your hard drive; this master folder will serve as the local root site folder as described in Lesson 03.

To install the Classroom in a Book files

1   Insert the Adobe Dreamweaver CS3 Classroom in a Book CD into your CD-ROM drive.

2   Create a folder on your hard disk.

3   Do one of the following:

•   Copy all the contents of the Lessons folder into the newly created folder.

•   Copy only the single lesson folder you need into the newly created folder.

Setting Preferences

To duplicate the experience in these lessons, make sure your Preferences are set correctly.

1   Start Adobe Dreamweaver CS3.

2   Choose Edit > Preferences (Windows) or Dreamweaver > Preferences (MacOS).

3   In the Preferences dialog box, click Accessibility in the Category list.

4   Clear all four checkboxes in the Show attributes when inserting area.

5   Click OK.

Additional resources

Adobe Dreamweaver CS3 Classroom in a Book is not meant to replace documentation that comes with the program. Only the commands and options used in the lessons are explained in this book.

For comprehensive information about program features, refer to these resources:

• Dreamweaver Help, which you can view by choosing Help > Dreamweaver Help.

• Training and support resources on the Adobe website (Adobe.com), which you can view by choosing Help > Help Resources Online if you have a connection to the Web.

• Adobe Design Center (http://www.adobe.com/designcenter/), where you can find a wealth of tips, tutorials, and other design inspiration and instructional content.

• The Adobe Dreamweaver CS3 Users Guide, which contains most of the material included in the Help system. If the Users Guide is not included in your Dreamweaver CS3 package, it is available for purchase at Adobe.com.

• Two bonus chapters are available to readers of the Adobe Dreamweaver CS3 Classroom in a Book: Increasing Productivity with Templates and Working with Code. Both chapters, in PDF format, and accompanying files are available from www.peachpit.com/dwcs3cib/.

Adobe Certification

The Adobe Training and Certification programs are designed to help Adobe customers and trainers improve and promote their product-proficiency skills. There are three levels of certification:

- Adobe Certified Expert (ACE)
- Adobe Certified Instructor (ACI)
- Adobe Authorized Training Center (AATC)

The Adobe Certified Expert program is a way for expert users to upgrade their credentials. You can use Adobe certification as a catalyst for getting a raise, finding a job, or promoting your expertise.

If you are an ACE-level instructor, the Adobe Certified Instructor programs takes your skills to the next level and gives you access to a wide range of Adobe resources. Adobe Authorized Training Centers offer instructor-led courses and training on Adobe products, employing only Adobe Certified Instructors. A directory of AATCs is available at http://partners.adobe.com. For information on the Adobe Certified programs, visit www.adobe.com/support/certification/main.html.

your vacation wonderland awaits...

Where you're royalty

Come enjoy the vacation of a lifetime! Stroll our sandy shores and swim in our calm cove—or enjoy a frisky romp in the vibrant surf. Take a break on the beach under our complimentary beach umbrellas and chairs. Here's just a few of the amenities you'll enjoy when you spend your vacation with us:

- ◆ Complimentary towels
- ◆ Doggie daycare provided
- ◆ 3 pools
- ◆ Hot tub
- ◆ Free beach umbrellas and chairs

Information – Contact Us

If you're new to Dreamweaver, your first question might be, "Where do I start?". The answer, in this book, is "right here." Take advantage of Dreamweaver's expertly designed starter pages to quickly create a standards-based layout, ready for your personalized content. Along the way, you'll explore how to work the Dreamweaver way and build a professional quality Web page.

1 | Quick Start to Dreamweaver CS3

In this lesson, you'll get introduced to Dreamweaver CS3 by building a sample Web page and by learning how to do the following:

- Create a new starter page.

- Save the document.

- Modify the page title.

- Change the text headings.

- Insert text from an external document.

- Add foreground and background images.

- Link to other pages in your site.

- Select and modify CSS styles.

- Preview your page in a browser.

This lesson will take about 90 minutes to complete. Be sure you have copied Lessons/Lesson01 from the Adobe Dreamweaver CS3 Classroom in a Book CD to your hard drive before beginning. As you work on this lesson, you'll overwrite the start files. If you need to restore the start files, copy them again from the CD.

Selecting a CSS starting point

Adobe Dreamweaver CS3 provides 32 different starting point files, all with different layouts. In this lesson, you'll create the starting point that you will be modifying throughout the lesson.

1   Start Adobe Dreamweaver CS3.

2   Choose File > New.

3   In the New Document dialog box, select the Blank Page category, if necessary, from the first column.

4   In the Page Type column, select HTML.

Dreamweaver does allow you to create a wide range of page types; HTML is the type commonly used for building standard Web pages.

5   In the Layout column, select two column fixed, left sidebar, header and footer, and the 12th sample layout in the list. The preview for this layout uses a padlock symbol to indicate that the width is set; other layouts allow for the width to expand or contract with the browser window.

6 Leave all other options at their default setting and click Create.

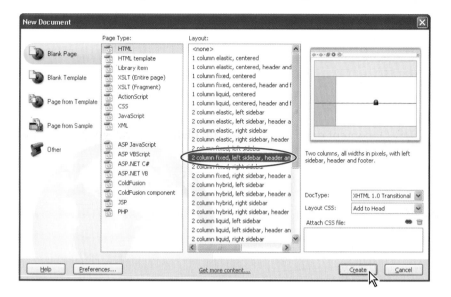

Your new page will appear in the Document window. If necessary, click Design to switch to Design view rather than Code or Split view.

Saving your page

Once you've created your page, it's a good idea to save it right away.

1 Choose File > Save. Alternatively, you can press Ctrl+S (Windows) or Cmd+S on (MacOS).

2 When the Save As dialog box appears, navigate to the Lesson01 folder and open it. In the File name field, enter **index.htm**. Click Save.

Modifying the page title

The page title on a Web page is displayed in the browser's title bar. Page titles are one of the key elements used by search engines like Google to index websites. It's important to always change Dreamweaver's default page title of Untitled Document to a pertinent phrase.

1   In the Title field of the Document toolbar, select the placeholder text, Untitled Document, and press Delete.

2   Enter **Vacation Palace** and press Enter (Windows) or Return (MacOS).

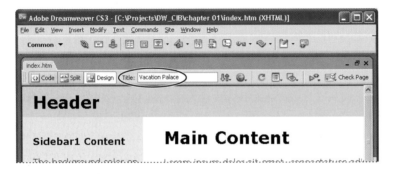

Changing headings

Placeholder headings are easily modified in Dreamweaver: by default, Dreamweaver is in text editing mode.

1   Double-click the placeholder text Header and enter the following phrase: **your vacation wonderland awaits...** . Dreamweaver provides a number of ways to select text that parallel word processing software, like double-clicking a single word.

2   Place your cursor in front of the placeholder text Main Content and drag it across the phrase. With the text selected, enter the following phrase: **Where you're royalty**. Use the click-and-drag method to select any range of text in Dreamweaver.

3   Choose File > Save.

Inserting text

Paragraph text is just as easy to update as heading text. In addition to manually entering text, Dreamweaver provides a robust engine for pasting text copied from other sources, like Microsoft Office products, while retaining as much of the formatting as desired.

1   Place your cursor in front of the placeholder text H2 level heading and drag it to the end of the following paragraph so that both the heading and paragraph are selected. Press Delete (Windows) or forward delete (MacOS) to remove the selection.

2   With Explorer (Windows) or Finder (MacOS), navigate to the CD files copied to your system and open lesson01 > vacation.rtf.

3   When the file opens, select all the text and press Ctrl+C (Windows) or Cmd+C (MacOS) to copy it to the clipboard.

4 In Dreamweaver, triple-click the placeholder paragraph below the header, Where you're royalty, and press Ctrl+V (Windows) or Cmd+V (MacOS) to paste the text from the clipboard.

Adding new images

Inserting images and graphics in Dreamweaver is very straightforward. Once on the page image properties, like alignment, can be adjusted through the Property inspector.

1 Select all the content in the sidebar, including the placeholder header Sidebar1 Content and the two subsequent paragraphs. Press Delete (Windows) or forward delete (MacOS) to remove the placeholder text.

2 In the Tag Selector, located at the bottom of the Document window, select <h3> and press Delete (Windows) or forward delete (MacOS) to remove the remaining HTML tag.

3 From the Common category of the Insert bar, click the Images menu button and choose Image from the list.

4　In the Select Image Source dialog box, navigate to the CD files copied to your system and select lesson01 > images > beach_birds_view.jpg. Click OK to confirm your choice.

5　Place your cursor at the start of second sentence in the main content paragraph that starts with the phrase "Stroll our…" and click Images in the Insert bar.

6　In the Select Image Source dialog box, select full_beach.jpg and click OK.

7　If the Property inspector is not visible, choose Window > Properties.

8　With the newly-inserted image selected, choose Right from the Align option list in the Property inspector. Text flows around images aligned to the left or right.

9　Choose File > Save.

Linking to other pages

Hyperlinks or, as they are more commonly known, links, are what makes the Web a unique medium. Dreamweaver makes it easy to create a link.

1   At the bottom of the page, select the placeholder text Footer and replace it with the phrase **Information – Contact Us.**

2   Double-click the word Information to select it. In the Property inspector, enter **information.htm** in the Link field. This link is intended to connect to a page in the same folder as the current document.

3   Select the phrase Contact Us and, in the Property inspector's Link field enter **http://www.yourvacationpalace.com/contact.htm**. By entering the full Web address, you can link directly to any accessible page on the Internet.

Selecting and modifying CSS styles

Modern Web pages use Cascading Style Sheets (CSS) for styling and layout. In this exercise, you'll modify the background color of the existing page, add a background graphic to a page section, and adjust various text attributes. All of these changes are accomplished through Dreamweaver's CSS Styles panel.

Changing background color of the page body

CSS can be used to alter the style properties of any given HTML tag, like <body>.

1   Choose Window > CSS Styles.

2   In the CSS Styles panel, click All to switch from Current mode, if necessary. All mode shows all the CSS styles associated with the page.

3   Expand the <style> entry in the All Rules pane by clicking the plus (Windows) or triangle (MacOS).

4   Select body and choose Edit Style, the pencil icon (✎) at the bottom of the CSS Styles panel.

5 When the CSS Rule definition for body dialog box appears, click the Background color swatch to open the pop-up color picker.

6 In the color picker, use the Eyedropper tool to sample the white color block in the second column.

Dreamweaver automatically inserts the hexadecimal value for white, #FFFFFF, in the Background color field.

7 Click OK to complete the change. Dreamweaver notes the new color in the Properties pane of the CSS Styles panel.

8 Press F4 to hide all panels; note that the background color has now changed from gray to white.

Standard background color   *Modified, white background*

9 Press F4 again to restore the panels.

10 Choose File > Save.

Inserting a graphic background

While foreground images are inserted directly onto the page, background images are placed through CSS.

1   Place your cursor anywhere in the header text, your vacation wonderland awaits.

2   From the Tag Selector, choose <div#header>. This selection indicates the <div> tag with an ID of #header.

3   In the CSS Styles panel, click Current to switch to Current mode.

4   From the Summary pane, click Background and then choose Edit Styles (✎).

5   When the CSS Rule definition for .twoColFixLtHdr #header dialog box appears, click the Browse button next to the Background image label and field.

6   In the Select Image Source dialog box, choose cloud_header.jpg in the images folder.

7 From the Repeat list, choose no-repeat. Click OK.

8 Click anywhere on the page to deselect the header and view the background image.

At this point, the black header text is a bit difficult to read against the sky blue background; you'll adjust the header text color in the next exercise.

Adjusting text fonts and colors

CSS gives you tremendous control over style selection. In addition to changing the look-and-feel of all the instances of a tag on a page or in an entire site, you can also target a style change to affect a tag in a particular location.

1   Place your cursor anywhere in the header text, your vacation wonderland awaits.

2   From the Tag Selector, choose <h1>.

3   In the CSS Styles panel, verify that Current mode is selected; if All mode is selected, click Current. If the About pane is displayed above the Properties pane, click Show Cascade (🖺), the icon on the far right of the About title bar.

4   In the Rules pane, choose .twoColFixLtHdr #header h1; click Edit Style (✏).

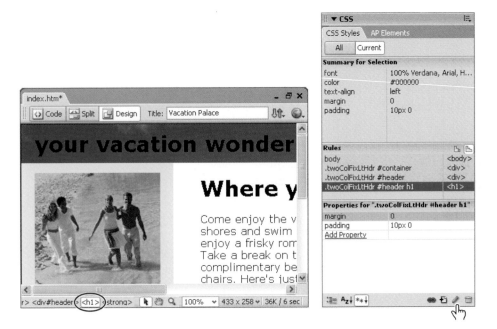

5   When the CSS Rules definition for .twoColFixLtHdr #header h1 appears, click Type in the Category column.

6 From the Font list, choose Geneva, Arial, Helvetica, sans-serif. Click the Color swatch to open the pop-up color picker and use the Eyedropper tool to select white in the second column. Click OK to confirm your changes.

CSS Rule definition for .twoColFixLtHdr #header h1

Category	Type
Type	
Background	Font: Geneva, Arial, Helvetica, sans-serif
Block	
Box	Size: [ ] pixels Weight: [ ]
Border	
List	Style: [ ] Variant: [ ]
Positioning	
Extensions	Line height: [ ] pixels Case: [ ]

Decoration: ☐ underline   Color: [ ] #FFFFFF
☐ overline
☐ line-through
☐ blink
☐ none

Help   OK   Cancel   Apply

7 Click anywhere on the page to deselect the header text.

The white header contrasts more sharply with the background image and is easier to read.

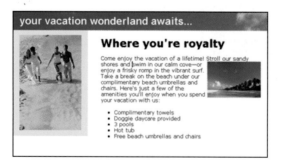

your vacation wonderland awaits...

Where you're royalty

Come enjoy the vacation of a lifetime! Stroll our sandy shores and swim in our calm cove—or enjoy a frisky romp in the vibrant surf. Take a break on the beach under our complimentary beach umbrellas and chairs. Here's just a few of the amenities you'll enjoy when you spend your vacation with us:

- Complimentary towels
- Doggie daycare provided
- 3 pools
- Hot tub
- Free beach umbrellas and chairs

Altering text size and spacing

In addition to changing the font style and color, as demonstrated in the previous exercise, you can also control text size and spacing with CSS.

1   Place your cursor anywhere in the main content heading or paragraph.

2   From the Tag Selector, choose <div#mainContent>.

3   With .twoColFixLtHdr #mainContent selected in the Rules pane of the CSS Styles panel, click Edit Style ( ).

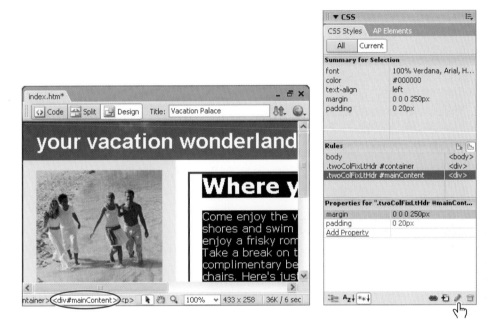

4   When the CSS Rules definition for .twoColFixLtHdr #mainContent appears, click Type in the Category column.

5   From the Size list, choose 14 and leave the default measurement unit set to pixels.

6   In the Line height field, enter **21** and again, leave the default measurement unit set to pixels. Click OK.

The paragraph now has a more open feel and your modifications to the page are now complete.

7   Choose File > Save.

Previewing your page in a browser

Although Dreamweaver does an excellent job of rendering Web pages in the Document window, it's important to always review your pages in one or more browsers. Dreamweaver allows you to preview in any locally installed browser, once defined in Preferences.

1   Choose File > Preview in Browser > Edit Browser List.

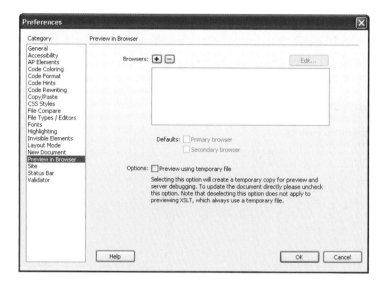

The Preferences dialog box appears, with the Preview in Browser category pre-selected.

2   Choose Add (⊞) to add a new browser to the list.

3   In the Add Browser dialog box, leave all fields blank and click Browse.

4   When the Select Browser dialog box opens, navigate to your preferred browser:

•   To choose Firefox on Windows, navigate to Program Files > Mozilla Firefox > firefox.exe.

•   To choose Internet Explorer on Windows, navigate to Program Files > Internet Explorer > iexplore.exe

•   To choose Safari on Macintosh, navigate to Applications: Safari.

5   Click Open to confirm your choice.

6 In the Name field of the Add Browser dialog box, enter the name you want to appear in the browser list, such as Firefox, Internet Explorer or Safari.

Note: Dreamweaver inserts the application file name which may not be the most user-friendly. Because of the ever-evolving nature of browsers, it's a good idea to combine your browser name with a version number like Firefox 2.0 or Internet Explorer 7.

7 Choose the Primary Browser option; click OK.

8 In the Preferences dialog box, click OK to complete the procedure.

9 Press F12 (Windows) or Option+F12 (MacOS) to preview the current page in your primary browser.

10 After you've completed your review of your new Web page, close your browser and return to Dreamweaver.

Congratulations—you've created your first Web page in Dreamweaver. As you can see, Dreamweaver combines substantial power with ease-of-use.

Review

▶ **Review questions**

1   What is the fastest way to create a starting layout design?

2   True or false: Any text pasted into Dreamweaver loses the original structure and formatting.

3   What's the difference between adding foreground and background images to the page?

4   How do the two modes of the CSS Styles panel—All and Current—differ?

▶ **Review answers**

1   Dreamweaver CS3 includes a large number of starting point files, available in the New Document dialog box, all of which use standards compliant, CSS-based layouts. Launch the New Document dialog box by choosing File > New.

2   False. Dreamweaver has the capacity to retain both the structure—paragraphs, lists, etc.—and formatting, including attributes such as bold and italic. As you'll learn in Lesson 4, Working with Text, you can choose the degree of structure and formatting kept.

3   Foreground images are inserted directly onto the page through the Images button on the Insert bar. Background images are added to the design through CSS.

4   The All mode displays a list of all styles associated with the current page, including those embedded in the <head> tag and those contained within external style sheets. The Current mode, on the other hand, shows details—such as rules, selectors and properties—pertaining to the current selection.

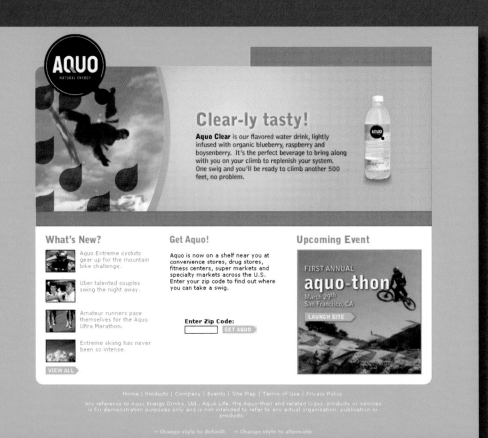

Although building Web pages involves a fair degree of technical expertise, Web designers are, in their hearts, artists—and all artists work best in their own workspace. Dreamweaver offers a great number of avenues for customizing the design experience and focusing your creative energies.

2 | Customizing your Workspace

In this lesson, you'll learn how to make the most of the Adobe Dreamweaver CS3 workspace and do the following :

- Understand the workspace layout.
- Arrange and reposition panels.
- Establish custom workspaces.
- Work with the Property inspector.
- Display and hide toolbars.
- Specify preferences.

This lesson will take about 90 minutes to complete. Be sure you have copied Lessons/Lesson02 from the Adobe Dreamweaver CS3 Classroom in a Book CD to your hard drive before beginning. As you work on this lesson, you'll overwrite the start files. If you need to restore the start files, copy them again from the CD.

Touring the workspace

In this exercise, you'll become more familiar with the basic elements of the Dreamweaver workspace, including the Welcome screen, the Document window, the Status bar and the panel groups.

Controlling the Welcome screen

The Welcome screen provides quick access to recent pages, easy creation for a range of page types and a direct connection to several key help topics. The Welcome screen appears when you first start the program and, optionally, when no other documents are open.

1 Start Adobe Dreamweaver CS3. In the Create New area of the Welcome screen, click HTML to open a new, blank page.

2 Choose File > Close.

Because no changes were made on the new page, Dreamweaver does not ask if you'd like to save it and the Welcome screen reappears.

3 In the Open a Recent Item area, click Open. When the Open dialog box is displayed, navigate to the Lesson02 folder copied from the CD to your system and select Lesson02 > example_page.html. Click Open.

The Open icon on the Welcome screen is a quick alternative to the File > Open menu command.

4   Choose File > Close. On the Welcome screen, in the Open a Recent Item area, click
the first entry, lesson02/example_page.html to reopen the file. Choose File > Close one
last time to return to the Welcome screen.

The Welcome screen is great for quickly opening recently modified pages; Dreamweaver
displays your last nine files; the Welcome screen on the Macintosh displays just the file
names, not the folder paths and the file names as seen here in the Windows Welcome
screen.

Note: *If you'd prefer not to work with the Welcome screen, click the Don't show again
option found in the lower left of the screen. Should you change your mind later, you can re-
enable the Welcome screen through an option in the General category of Preferences.*

Choosing your Document window

Most Web authoring in Dreamweaver takes place in the Document window. The Document window offers three different views:

- Design view – Renders the Web page like a browser.
- Code view – Displays the page's source code.
- Split view – Combines both Design and Code view.

The three views are tightly connected: any changes made to the page in Design view are instantly viewable in Code view, and vice versa.

1   From the Open a Recent Item area of the Welcome screen, click lesson02/example_ page.html. In the paragraph below the Get Aquo heading, select the phrase on a shelf including the space following shelf.

Dreamweaver defaults to opening files in Design view, but any selections you make are also made in Code view.

2   In the Document toolbar, located directly above the Document window, click Code view (⬚). Press Delete (Windows) or forward delete (MacOS) to remove the selected phrase. Click Design view (⬚) to return to the rendered page and review the change.

Sometimes, it's helpful to see both the rendered page and the source code simultaneously as you can in Split view.

3   Click Split view (⬚) in the Document toolbar. Position your cursor on the border between the source code and the rendered document until you see the horizontal border cursor (⬚). Drag the border so that the two views are equally visible.

4 In the design section of the Document window, select the newly entered phrase near you and change it to nearby you. Note that the modification is automatically applied to the code.

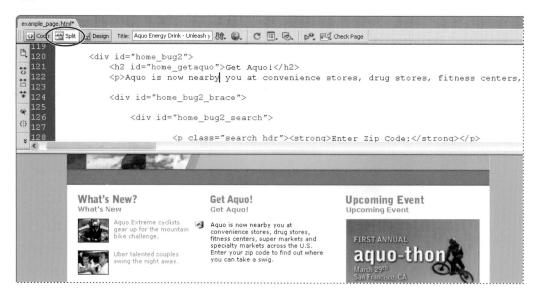

5 In the code section of the Document window, select the phrase nearby you and press Delete (Windows) or forward delete (MacOS). Note that the design section is not automatically updated. Click anywhere in the design section to confirm your code changes and update the page. Click Design view.

6 Choose File > Save. Leave the current file open for the next section if you are continuing the lesson; otherwise, click File > Close.

When you're working in the code, Dreamweaver waits to make sure you've completed your modifications before refreshing the design. You can signal you're done by clicking in the design section or by choosing Refresh Design View (⟳) from the Document toolbar.

Using the Status bar

The Status bar is located at the bottom of the Document window and contains some of Dreamweaver's most useful features. In this exercise, you'll explore the Tag Selector and the Zoom controls.

1   If you closed the file from the previous exercise, choose File > Open Recent > example_file.html.

2   Place your cursor anywhere in the text on the left-side of the page that reads: Aquo Extreme cyclists gear up for the mountain bike challenge.

The Tag Selector shows a series of tags nearest to the current cursor position. The right-most tag in the Tag Selector—in this example, <a>—is the tag immediately surrounding the cursor.

3   In the Tag Selector, select the <a> tag. Note the corresponding selection in the Document window. Next, select the tag to the immediate left, <div.home_bug_desc>. Note the expanded selection. Continue to select each tag in the Tag Selector in turn.

The Tag Selector is extremely useful for pinpointing exactly what you want to modify and precisely represents the hierarchical nature of HTML where one tag is nested within another.

While the Tag Selector is great for targeting a specific section of code, the Status bar offers another feature for a more visual approach: the Zoom tool.

4　From the Status bar, click the Zoom tool (🔍). With the magnifying glass cursor, click once on the top image in left column. Click one more to zoom into the page more.

The Zoom tool increases the magnification of the page from 100% to 150% with the first click. With each subsequent click, the magnification increases according to the values in the Set Magnification list, also found on the Status Bar.

5　Press Alt (Windows) or Opt (MacOS) and click on the image again to reduce the magnification; the plus sign in the Zoom tool cursor changes to a minus sign. Note that the entry in the Set Magnification list changes with each click and now shows 150%. From the Set Magnification list, choose 100%.

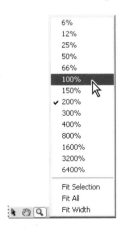

The Zoom tool can also expand a selected area to its highest magnification.

6   Move your cursor to the upper left corner of the top image in the left column and drag out a rectangle to surround the top three images and their adjacent paragraphs. When you release your mouse button, Dreamweaver magnifies the selected area as much as possible for the current Document window. Double-click the Select tool (⬉) in the Status bar to return to 100% magnification and Select mode.

> *Like some other graphic programs, including Adobe Photoshop and Adobe Fireworks, you can also double-click the Zoom tool to set the magnification at 100%, but you'll still be in Zoom mode. It's much quicker to accomplish both tasks at the same time by double-clicking the Select tool.*

The Set Magnification list includes other options besides specific zoom levels:

• Fit Selection – Zooms in on the current selection to the greatest magnification possible.

• Fit All – Displays the entire page in the Document window.

• Fit Width – Adjusts the magnification to show the full width of the page.

You'll find two other useful bits of information on the Status bar, immediately to the right of the Set Magnification list: the dimensions of the current Document window and the approximate file weight of the page and corresponding download times. Use the Window Size pop-up list to resize the Document window; if the Document window is maximized, the Window Size options will not be available. Download times are calculated assuming an Internet connection speed specified in the Status Bar category of Preferences.

Adjusting panels and panel groups

Panels, in Dreamweaver, target specific Web page or site elements, such as CSS styles or the server-side code. Related panels are arranged in panel groups, which can be reconfigured or repositioned on the page as desired. In this exercise, you'll learn how to work with panel and panel groups and customize them to best fit your workflow.

1   If you closed the file from the previous exercise, choose File > Open Recent > example_file.html.

Managing panel groups in Windows

In Windows, panel groups are initially docked to the right side of the Document window. The entire panel group collection can be quickly collapsed by clicking the border button. The border button displays a right-facing triangle when the panel groups are open and a left-facing triangle when they are closed. Widen or narrow the width of the docked panel groups by dragging the border in the desired direction; a horizontal two-headed arrow appears when your cursor is in the right position for dragging the border.

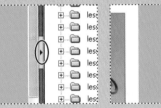

Border button with right-facing triangle when open   *Border button with left-facing triangle when closed*

Maximize your Document window by collapsing all the panel groups with a single click.

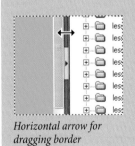

Horizontal arrow for dragging border

2   If you do not see the Files panel, choose Window > Files.

Alternatively, you can press F8 to open or close the Files panel.

3   Collapse the Files panel group by clicking its name, Files, in the panel title bar. Click the name again to reopen it.

The individual panels in each panel group are accessible through their tabs; you can use the tabs to re-arrange the panels within a group.

4   In the Files panel group, click Assets to display the Assets panel. Click Snippets
to display the Snippets panel. Drag the Snippets panel tab in between the Files and
Assets tabs; note the rearranged tabs in the panel group. Restore the Snippets panel to
its original position by dragging its tab to the right of the Assets panel. Click Files to
display that panel.

5   Click CSS Styles to open the CSS Styles panel. With two or more panels open, you can adjust the height of an individual panel. Position your cursor at the bottom of the CSS Styles panel; when you see a two-headed vertical arrow (↕), drag down to expose more of the CSS Styles panel. Place your cursor in the Files panel title bar until the two-headed vertical arrow appears and drag up to show more of the Files panel.

In addition to variably changing the height of individual panels, you can expand a single panel to the maximum height.

6   Double-click the CSS Styles panel title bar to maximize the CSS Styles panel; double-click the title bar of the Files panel to maximize the Files panel.

Although the panel groups are thematically organized, the default groupings may not match your workflow. Dreamweaver panels can be regrouped or, for the most part, isolated, as desired.

7   First, choose Window > Frames and then choose Window > History to open their respective individual panels. From the Frames panel Options menu (≡▾), located on the far right of the panel title bar, choose Groups Frames with > History.

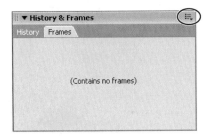

You'll notice that the new panel group has been automatically renamed to History & Frames. While this name is perfectly adequate, you may want to customize it. Renaming a file group is very straightforward.

8   From the History & Frames panel group Options menu, choose Rename panel group. When the Rename Panel Group dialog box opens, change History & Frames to History and Frames; click OK when you're done.

In addition to changing how panels are grouped, it's also possible to ungroup a panel completely.

9 Drag the Frames panel from the History and Frames panel group and drop it in the Document window area. Reposition the panel on the screen by dragging the title bar to a new location.

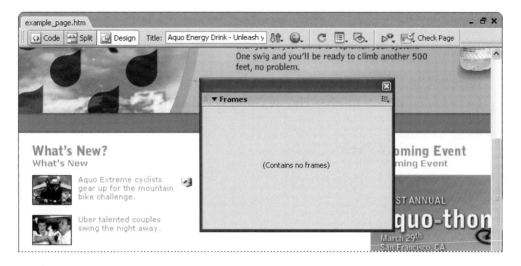

While occasionally, you might find it useful to isolate individual panels in the work area, most designers find it beneficial to keep panels in the panel group area. To return a panel to the panel group, you'll need to drag the panel by a special location on the title bar.

If you're using a dual monitor work environment, you can drag your panels or panel groups to the secondary monitor.

10 Move your cursor over the top left of the Frames panel title bar until the 4-headed arrow (on the Mac, it's a hand icon) appears; this portion of the title bar is designated by two columns of dots and is known as the gripper. Drag the Frames gripper to the panel groups above the History panel until a thick black line appears and then drop the Frames panel.

Drag the gripper to move panels   The thick black line indicates the panel is ready to be docked.

💡 *You can also drag panel groups by the gripper to reposition them above or below other panel groups.*

The Frames panel is back in its original position. Many designers find it helpful to remove less frequently used panels from the panel groups collection until they are needed; there are a couple of ways to accomplish this task.

11 From the Frames panel Options menu, choose Close panel group. Right-click (Windows) or Control-click (MacOS) anywhere in the History panel and choose Close panel group from the pop-up menu.

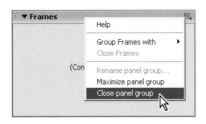

12 Choose File > Close.

Creating custom workspaces

Once you've created the ideal workspace for yourself, you can save your configuration and return to it at any time. In addition, Dreamweaver provides a couple of workspace layouts, include the default, that can be easily reinstated.

1   From the Applications panel Options menu, choose Close panel group.

In this exercise, you'll save a slightly customized workspace; the Applications panel group was closed to differentiate the current workspace from the default one.

2   Choose Window > Workspace Layout > Save Current. When the Save Workspace Layout dialog box appears, enter MySpace in the Name field and click OK.

3   Choose Window > Workspace Layout > Designer (Windows) or Window > Workspace Layout >Default (MacOS).

The original workspace is restored.

Note: The Workspace Layout options are different for Windows and MacOS. On Windows, the initial available layouts are Coder (where the panels are on the left), Designer and Dual Screen. With MacOS, the options are Default (same as Designer) and Dual Screen.

4   Choose Window > Workspace Layout > MySpace.

You'll note that the Applications panel group has been restored. Let's return to the default layout to continue our exploration of the Dreamweaver workspace.

5   Choose Window > Workspace Layout > Designer (Windows) or Window > Workspace Layout >Default (MacOS).

Using the Property inspector

Although Dreamweaver's Property inspector is, essentially, another panel, it deserves special mention for its flexibility and central place in the Web designer's workflow. The options available in the Property inspector change according to the current selection. By default, the Text Property inspector is shown with tools available for applying formats and adjusting text alignment. If an image is selected, the Property inspector displays the height and width values as well as links to image processing tools. In this exercise, you'll learn how to open and close the Property inspector and use some of its more common interface elements.

1   If you closed the file from the earlier exercise, choose File > Open Recent > example_file.html.

2   If you don't see the Property inspector at the bottom of the Document window, choose Window > Properties.

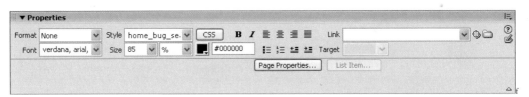

3   (Windows only) Click the Properties label in the Property inspector title bar once to minimize the Property inspector; click Properties again to restore the inspector.

Note: Window users will notice that a collapse/expand button, similar to the one on the panel groups is located on the border above the Property inspector. These buttons hide or reveal the Property inspector, which can either be open or closed.

4 Select the phrase Enter zip code in the middle of the page. In the Property inspector, click the B (for Bold) button to deselect it and click I (for Italic).

to find out where you can take a
swig.

Enter Zip Code:

GET AQUO

▼ Properties
Format Paragraph   Style search_hdr   CSS **B** *I*
Font verdana, arial,   Size 85   %   #000000
                                    Page Properties...

Note: The Property inspector uses the B and I buttons as shorthand for the resulting effects. The actual tags inserted to achieve those effects are <strong> for bold and <em>, short for emphasis, for italic.

Some controls on the Property inspector, like the bold and italic buttons, are toggles: click once to enable and again to disable. An enabled toggle appears recessed as if the button has been pushed in.

5 Click the Text Color swatch and, when the pop-up color picker is displayed, choose the red sample in the middle of the second column with the Eyedropper tool. Click anywhere, either from the color swatches or anywhere on the screen, to see the color change.

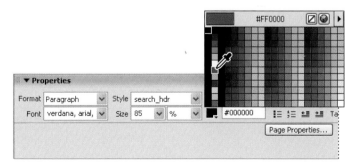

#FF0000

▼ Properties
Format Paragraph   Style search_hdr
Font verdana, arial,   Size 85   %   #000000
                                    Page Properties...

Color swatches are a common user interface element in Dreamweaver; you'll find them in various Property inspectors as well as other panels and dialog boxes.

6   Click Page Properties in the lower portion of the Property inspector. When the Page Properties dialog box appears, from the Size list choose large. Click Apply to see the effect on the page. Reverse this change by choosing small from the Size list and clicking OK.

Page Properties   ⊠

Category	Appearance
Appearance	
Links	
Headings	
Title/Encoding	
Tracing Image	

Page font: verdana, arial, helvetica, sans-serif ⌄ **B** *I*

Size: large ⌄ pixels ⌄

Text color: ■ #000000

Background color: ▨ #8cc63f

Background image: Browse...

Repeat: ⌄

Left margin: 0 pixels ⌄   Right margin: 0 pixels ⌄

Top margin: 0 pixels ⌄   Bottom margin: 0 pixels ⌄

Help   OK   Cancel   Apply

The Property inspector often includes buttons that launch dialog boxes to handle more wide-ranging modifications. Some buttons or other user interface controls on the Property inspector are inactive until your cursor is placed in a relevant element. For example, List item (located to the right of Page Properties) remains disabled until your cursor is placed in a bulleted, numbered, or other type of list.

7 Select the top image in the left column and note that the Property inspector changes with your selection. In the Alt field, enter the phrase Aquo Extreme Cyclist and press Tab.

As you work through this book, you'll notice that Dreamweaver offers many different kinds of Property inspectors, like those for text and graphics.

8 Choose File > Save.

Adjusting toolbars

Dreamweaver toolbars bring point-and-click ease to many common Web authoring operations: inserting page elements, such as tables or images; performing operations like putting or getting files; and switching modes, as when changing from Design view to Code view. There are four separate toolbars:

• Document – Includes the three view options (Design, Code and Split), the page title field and other page-oriented options

• Insert – Adds many different elements to the Web page. The Insert bar is divided into seven categories.

- Standard – Offers traditional file operations—such as Open, Save, Undo, and Cut/Copy/Paste—as well as some Dreamweaver specific features, such as Print Code and Browse in Bridge.

- Style Rendering – Controls the CSS media type rendered in the Document window. The Style Rendering toolbar makes it easy, for example, to design a print style sheet.

In this exercise, you'll focus on general toolbar interactions and the most frequently used toolbar, the Insert bar. The other toolbars are covered in other lessons in their respective context.

1   If you closed the file from the earlier exercise, choose File > Open Recent > example_file.html.

Dreamweaver toolbars require that a page be open to be enabled.

Initially, only the Insert and Document toolbar are shown. You can reveal the other toolbars in a number of ways.

2   Choose View > Toolbars > Standard. Note that the Standard toolbar appears above the Document toolbar. Right-click (Windows) or Control-click (MacOS) on the Standard toolbar; in the pop-up menu, choose Standard again (now with a checkmark next to it) to hide the toolbar.

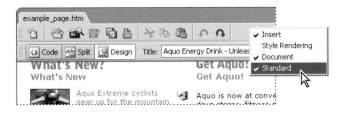

Right-clicking or Control-clicking in any toolbar, not just Standard, displays the list of available toolbars.

As noted earlier, the Insert bar is divided into numerous categories. You can view these categories in one of two ways: a menu list or tabs.

3   If your Insert bar displays the available categories as a series of tabs, select the Insert bar Options menu and choose Show as Menu.

Note: To revert to a tabbed interface, choose Show as Tabs from the category list. All figures in this book displaying the Insert bar show the categories as a menu, but you're free to use either tabs or menus.

4   From the Common category, drag the Hyperlink object onto the page and drop it after the main paragraph that ends …take a swig.

Objects can either be dragged to a specific location on the page, or you can place your cursor where you'd like your object to appear and click the Insert bar object once.

5   When the Hyperlink dialog box opens, enter the phrase More info… in the Text field and info.html in the Link field. Click OK when you're done.

Some objects, like Hyperlink, display a dialog box so you can define the required parameters. Other objects simply insert the necessary code for the requested item.

6   From the Insert bar category list, choose Text.

7 Place your cursor directly after the word Aquo in the phrase that starts Aquo is now at convenience stores. From the Characters menu button, located at the far right of the Insert bar, choose TM.

| Text ▼ | **B** | *I* | **S** | *em* | ¶ | [""] | PRE | **h1** | **h2** | **h3** | **ul** | **ol** | **li** | **dl** | **dt** | **dd** | abbr. | W3C | TM ▼ |

Get Aquo!
Get Aquo!

Aquo is now at convenience stores, drug stores, fitness centers, super markets and specialty markets across the U.S. Enter your zip code to find out where you can take a swig. More info...

Enter Zip Code:

Get Aquo!
Get Aquo!

Aquo™ is now at convenience stores, drug stores, fitness centers, super markets and specialty markets across the U.S. Enter your zip code to find out where you can take a swig. More info...

Enter Zip Code:

In addition to single objects, the Insert bar includes a number of menu buttons, identifiable by the down-pointing triangle to the right of the object. Menu buttons initially display a generic object icon which does not insert any code; you must select an object from the list to add it to the page. Dreamweaver remembers the last selected item from a menu button and places it at the top of the menu. For example, the TM object is now the top entry in the Characters menu button and can be reapplied with a single click.

The large number of object available in all the Dreamweaver toolbars can be overwhelming. Dreamweaver provides a method for displaying your most commonly-used objects in a special category, Favorites.

8 Switch to the Favorites category of the Insert bar. Right-click (Windows) or Control-click (MacOS) on the Insert bar and choose Customize Favorites. When the Favorites dialog box appears, select Table from the Available objects list on the left and click Move (⊡) to designate it as a Favorite object. Scroll down the list and repeat the same operation for Image.

Because there are so many objects, Dreamweaver allows you to specify a category to limit the selection.

9 From the Available objects list, choose Text. In the list of Text objects, select Copyright and click Move. Repeat the same operation with Trademark.

You can use the Up and Down buttons and the Separator option to customize the look and feel of your Favorites category.

10 In the Favorite objects list, select Image and click Up (▲). Select Table and click Separator. When you're done, click OK.

Objects higher on the list of favorites in the dialog box appear to the left in the toolbar. The separator adds a vertical rule to indicate a new group.

Personalizing Preferences

Dreamweaver Preferences give you complete control over your Web authoring experience, from the Welcome screen to the code Dreamweaver generates. Most Preferences take effect immediately after being modified; there's no need to restart the program. In this exercise, you'll learn how to access Preferences, review a few key categories, and make changes to better fit your workflow.

1   Choose Edit > Preferences (Windows) or Dreamweaver > Preferences (MacOS).

2   When the Preferences dialog box opens, make sure the General category is displayed; if it is not, select General from the Category list on the left of the dialog box.

The General preferences offer both general document and editing options. In the Document section, you may, for example, choose to show or hide the Welcome screen.

3   If the Reopen documents on startup option is not checked, select it.

With this option enabled, any files left open when your last Dreamweaver session ended are automatically reopened the next time Dreamweaver is launched.

4   In the the Maximum number of history steps field, change from 50 to 100.

Dreamweaver regards each action you take—except for moves and selections with the cursor—as a history step. The more history steps you have available, the more actions you can undo.

5   Select the Copy/Paste category and choose the Text with structure plus full formatting option.

The Copy/Paste category settings affect material copied from other applications, like Microsoft Word, and pasted into Dreamweaver using the standard Paste command. Choosing this option retains the highest degree of fidelity to the source material in Dreamweaver.

6   Select the Invisible Elements category and, if not already selected, enable the Comments and Line Breaks options. Click OK when you're done.

Dreamweaver employs a series of icons called Invisible Elements to mark the existence of Web page markup not typically rendered in the browser; the options set in this category determine whether the icon is displayed in the Document window if the markup exists on the page.

As you can see, there are many categories and settings in Dreamweaver Preferences. You'll encounter many of these options in the other lessons throughout this book.

Review

▶ **Review questions**

1 True or False: The Welcome screen is just a pretty picture and has no real functionality.

2 Name and briefly describe the three Dreamweaver views available in the Document window.

3 What is the function of the Tag Selector on the Status Bar?

4 True or False: There's no way to preserve your custom workspace arrangements.

5 What's the best way to customize the Insert bar?

▶ **Review answers**

1 False. The Dreamweaver Welcome screen provides quick access to recently opened files, new file types and new sites.

2 Design view, which renders the current Web page like a browser; Code view, which displays the page's source code; and Split view, which shows both Design and Code views.

3 The Tag Selector shows the tags surrounding the current selection. Users can select an item from the Tag Selector to select a corresponding tag.

4 False. Choose Window > Workspace Layout > Save Current to store the present workspace layout.

5 Right-click (Windows) or Control-click (MacOS) on any toolbar and choose Customize Favorites and specify objects to place in the Favorites category of the Insert bar.

dev/design

Home   Spirit   Folks   Work   Contact

Better by design

Your visions are our reality

Lorem ipsum dolor sit amet, consetetur sadipscing elitr, sed diam nonumy eirmod tempor invidunt ut labore et dolore magna aliquyam erat, sed diam voluptua. At vero eos et accusam et justo duo dolores et ea rebum. Stet clita kasd gubergren, no sea takimata sanctus est Lorem ipsum dolor sit amet..

Top dogs sleep here

Lorem ipsum dolor sit amet, consetetur sadipscing elitr, sed diam nonumy eirmod tempor invidunt ut labore et dolore magna aliquyam erat, sed diam voluptua.

Paradigms shifted here

At vero eos et accusam et justo duo dolores et ea rebum. Stet clita kasd gubergren, no sea takimata sanctus est Lorem ipsum dolor sit amet. Stet clita kasd gubergren, no sea takimata sanctus est Lorem ipsum dolor sit amet..

Learn more about our spirit »

Company Anon

Company Anon needed a full commercial facelift. Lorem ipsum dolor sit amet, consetetur sadipscing elitr, sed diam nonumy eirmod tempor invidunt ut labore et dolore magna aliquyam erat, sed diam voluptua. At vero eos et accusam et justo duo dolores et ea rebum. Stet clita kasd gubergren, no sea takimata sanctus est Lorem ipsum dolor sit amet.

Lorem ipsum dolor sit amet, consetetur sadipscing elitr, sed diam nonumy eirmod tempor invidunt ut labore et dolore magna aliquyam erat, sed diam voluptua. At vero eos et accusam et justo duo dolores et ea rebum. Stet clita kasd gubergren, no sea takimata sanctus est Lorem ipsum dolor sit amet

Learn more about our work »

Cascading Style Sheets (CSS) are the technology used by modern Web designers to provide a consistent look-and-feel across a site. Dreamweaver CS3 is a true CSS power tool with the ability to easily display, define, apply and modify styles for a variety of mediums, including: screen, print and handheld devices.

3 | Applying Cascading Style Sheets

In this lesson, you'll learn how to work with Cascading Style Sheets (CSS) in Dreamweaver and do the following :

- Define a Dreamweaver site.
- Attach an external style sheet.
- Make a new CSS style rule.
- Apply a style to your page.
- Change existing CSS properties.
- Create a print style sheet.

This lesson will take about 90 minutes to complete. Be sure you have copied Lessons/Lesson03 from the Adobe Dreamweaver CS3 Classroom in a Book CD to your hard drive before beginning. As you work on this lesson, you'll overwrite the start files. If you need to restore the start files, copy them again from the CD.

Defining a Dreamweaver site

Starting with this chapter, the remaining lessons in this book work within a Dreamweaver site. In Dreamweaver, you work with a local site located in a folder on your system and a remote site, stored on your Web host's computer. The two sites are essentially mirrors of each other in their folder structure and files. In this exercise, you'll set up your local site.

1   Start Adobe Dreamweaver CS3.

2   Choose Site > New Site. When the Site Definition dialog box appears, click the Advanced tab to switch to the Advanced view, if necessary.

The Basic view of the Site Definition dialog box, while less technical, does require more preliminary information. By using the Advanced view, you'll be able to set just the part of the site definition you need to get started.

3   In the Local Info category of the Site Definition dialog box, enter **DW CIB** in the Site name field and press Tab.

💡 *Site names are listed in the Files panel and are typically related to a particular project or client.*

4 Click the folder icon next to the Local root folder field. When the Choose local root folder for site DW CIB dialog box opens, navigate to the folder containing the lessons copied from the Adobe Dreamweaver CS3 Classroom in a Book CD to your hard drive and click Select.

5 In the Site Definition dialog box, click OK to confirm your choices.

Now that a site has been set up, you can easily open files from within Dreamweaver.

Previewing your completed file

To get a sense of the file you will work on in this session, let's preview the completed page in the browser.

1 In the Files panel, expand the Lesson03 folder.

2 Select the home_final.htm file and press F12 (Windows) or Option+F12 (MacOS).

3   Preview the page in your primary browser; note the layout and various styles applied to the text—all created by CSS styles.

Note: Although both the links in the navigation bar and those within the page do not connect to any other pages, they are interactive and will change when your cursor hovers over them.

4   In your browser, choose File > Print Preview (Windows) or File > Print and then choose Preview (MacOS). Note the different elements and layout, more suitable for the printer than the screen. Close the Print Preview window.

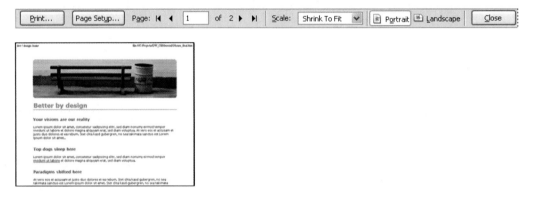

5   Close your browser and return to Dreamweaver.

Attaching an external style sheet

In modern Web design, it is considered a best practice to keep the vast majority of your CSS styles in an external style sheet. Typically, all of the pages in a site link to a single style sheet, which allows a single style change—like changing the color of an <h1> tag—to affect an entire site. Dreamweaver provides a very straightforward way to attach an external style sheet to Web pages.

1   If the Files panel is not on the screen, choose Window > Files. In the Files panel, double-click lesson03 > home.htm to open the page in the Document window.

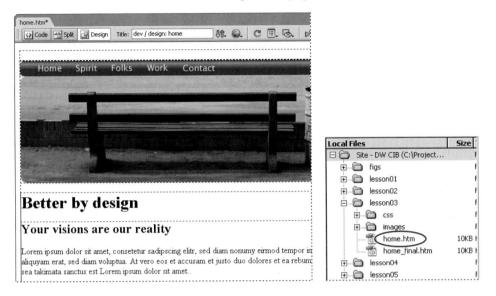

As you can see, the page has basic content—images, headings and paragraphs—but no real layout or style. In this exercise, the entire layout and a good portion of the styles have been previously created and are stored in an external style sheet. The next task is to attach the external style sheet to the current page.

2   Choose Window > CSS Styles. In the CSS Styles panel, click Attach Style Sheet (⊛), the chain link icon at the bottom of the panel.

3   When the Attach External Style Sheet dialog box opens, click Browse. In the Select Style Sheet File dialog box, navigate to the lesson03 > css folder and select main.css. Click OK (Windows) or Choose (MacOS) when you're done.

4   In the Attach External Style Sheet dialog box, verify that the Add as: Link option is selected. From the Media list, choose screen. Click Preview to make sure that you've selected the proper CSS file; when you're done, click OK.

Note: Modern CSS allows for different media types, like screen, handheld and print. In this exercise, you chose to attach the external style sheet for the screen medium; later in this lesson, you'll attach another style sheet for the print medium.

As you can see, the page is changed significantly. A logo appears at the top of the page, most of the headings and paragraphs are now styled and the lower portion of the page is now in two columns.

5   Choose File > Save. Press F12 (Windows) or Option+F12 (MacOS) to preview page in your primary browser. When you're done, close your browser and return to Dreamweaver.

In the next exercise, you'll learn how to create new style rules for your newly-attached style sheet.

Creating new CSS rules

A CSS rule is comprised of two primary parts: selector and properties. For example, the following CSS rule, the selector is the tag h1 and the properties are color: red and font-size: 36px:

```
h1 {
  color: red;
  font-size: 36px;
}
```

In Dreamweaver, you can create new CSS styles in a point-and-click environment and Dreamweaver will write the proper code for you. Dreamweaver gives you the ability to define CSS rules for any type of selector. In this exercise, you'll create rules for two different selector types: one for an HTML tag and the other for a custom CSS selector called a *class*.

Defining styles for tags

CSS style rules which target specific tags are immediately and automatically applied whenever the tag is used. For example, in this exercise, you'll create a rule for the <h1> tag that changes the color to a bright orange, among other modifications. After this rule is defined, the text within any <h1> tag will be the same color for any page applying the same external style sheet.

1 If necessary, re-open the home.htm file worked on in previous exercise by double-clicking its entry in the Files panel.

2 In the CSS Styles panel, make sure the panel is in All mode; if the panel is in Current mode, click All. Click the plus sign (Windows) or triangle (MacOS) next to the main.css entry to expand it.

3 Click New CSS Rule (⊞), located at the bottom of the CSS Styles panel.

4 When the New CSS Rule dialog box opens, choose the Selector Type: Tag option. From the Tag list, choose h1; alternatively, you can enter h1 into the Tag field. Make sure that the Define in: option is set to main.css and click OK.

💡 *Dreamweaver initially inserts the selector associated with the current cursor location in the Selector field, a feature that is very useful when creating advanced selectors. In such situations, it's helpful to place your cursor in the portion of the page for which you're creating a style rule.*

5   In the CSS Rule Definition for h1 in main.css dialog box, make sure the Type category is selected; if not, choose Type from the list of categories on the left of the dialog box. From the Font list, choose Verdana, Arial, Helvetica, sans-serif. In the Size field, enter **1.9**, then press Tab and choose **ems** from the list. In the Color field, enter **#EE9414**.

Dreamweaver divides the available CSS properties into eight different categories. Properties in the Type category affect the text aspect of the selector.

6   Click the Box category. In the Padding area, deselect the Same for all checkbox. In the Bottom field, enter **3** and press Tab.

The Box category controls the invisible box surrounding selectors by specifying values for its width, height, padding and margins, among other properties. If the design called for the same amount of padding around the selector, you would have left the Same of all checkbox selected and entered a value in the Top field, which would have been applied to Right, Bottom, and Left as well.

7 Click the Border category. Deselect all three Same for all checkboxes. In the Style column of the Bottom row, choose solid from the list; in the Width column of the Bottom row, enter **2** in the field and press Tab to accept the default pixels measurement unit; and, in the Color column of the Bottom row, enter **#A7A37E**. Click OK when you're done.

Note: A second file, main.css, is opened behind the current document. Because you are making changes to the external CSS file, Dreamweaver opens it. To undo a change to an external style sheet, you'll need to switch to the open file and choose Edit > Undo.

The newly-defined style is immediately applied to the <h1> tag near the top of the page, Better by design. The text's font, size, and color are all affected, a small bit of padding is added to the bottom of the text as is a full-width border.

You may have noticed that the new rule was added to the bottom of the All Rules list; this list reflects the order of the CSS code. Designers often like to group related styles to make it easier to find them; you can quickly move any style to a different location and Dreamweaver will rewrite the code for you.

8 In the CSS Styles panel, select the newly-added style, h1, and drag it above the h2 entry.

9 Choose File > Save All to store changes to both the HTML and CSS files.

Setting up custom classes

Unlike with tag styles, not all CSS rules are automatically applied. In this next part of the exercise, you'll create a custom selector called a class which is intended to be applied as needed.

1 If necessary, re-open the home.htm file worked on in previous exercise by double-clicking its entry in the Files panel.

2 From the bottom of the CSS Styles panel, click New CSS Rule.

3 When the New CSS Rule dialog box appears, choose the Selector Type: Class option and in the Name field, enter **.more**—be sure to include the leading period. Verify that the Define in field is set to main.css and click OK.

4   In the CSS Rule Definition for .more in main.css dialog box, click Block in the Category list. From the Text align list, choose center and click OK.

5   Choose File > Save All.

Other than another entry added to the All Rules list in the CSS Styles panel, you won't notice any change in Dreamweaver. Because this rule uses a class selector, it must be manually applied—a step described in the next exercise.

Applying styles

Dreamweaver provides a variety of methods for applying a style to a tag. In this exercise, you'll use two of the approaches: one using the Property inspector and the other using the Tag Selector.

1   If necessary, re-open the home.htm file worked on in previous exercise by double-clicking its entry in the Files panel.

2 Place your cursor in the phrase, Learn more about our spirit. In the Tag Selector, choose <p>.

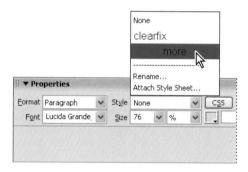

3 If necessary, press Ctrl+F3 (Windows) or Cmd+F3 (MacOS) to open the Property inspector.

4 From the Style list of the Property inspector, choose more.

Note: The Property inspector's Style list, which displays the available CSS classes in a document, replicates particular characteristics of the style—including relative size, color and alignment—to make it easier for you to find the desired style.

Note that the paragraph is now center aligned and that the indicator in the Tag Selector now includes the style: <p.more>

A slightly faster technique of applying CSS styles uses just the Tag Selector.

5 Place your cursor in the text at the bottom of the right column, Learn more about our work ».

6 In the Tag Selector, Right-click (Windows) or Control+click (MacOS) <p> and, from the pop-up menu, choose Set Class > more.

7 Choose File > Save.

Changing properties

CSS styles are rarely set in stone: adjustments are likely throughout the Web site creation process. Dreamweaver gives direct, editable access to the properties of any defined CSS style in the Properties pane of the CSS Styles panel.

1 If necessary, re-open the home.htm file worked on in previous exercise by double-clicking its entry in the Files panel.

2 In the CSS Styles panel, select .more from the All Rules list.

3 In the Properties pane, located below the All Rules list, select the existing text-align property value, center. Expand the drop-down list and choose right.

The two paragraphs with the .more class applied are immediately affected.

4 Choose File > Save All.

The more you work with Dreamweaver, the more you'll find yourself applying the skills learned in the preceding exercises: creating new CSS rules, applying custom classes and changing rule properties.

In the next exercise, you'll learn how to convert a style sheet developed for the screen into one for the print medium.

Developing a Print style sheet

A key concept of modern Web design is the separation of presentation (CSS) from content (the HTML tags, text and other page elements). Because of this presentation, CSS files can present the content for a specific medium; for example, the style sheet applied in the previous exercises was designed to be shown on a computer screen. In this exercise, you'll learn how to convert a CSS file for screen to one for print.

Saving and attaching a print style sheet

Although you can develop a print style sheet from scratch, it's usually much faster to convert an existing screen style sheet. The first step is to save the existing external style sheet under a new name.

1   If necessary, re-open main.css by double-clicking on its entry in the Files panel, located in the lesson03 > css folder.

2   Choose File > Save As. When the Save As dialog box opens, enter **print.css** in the File name field and click Save.

3   If necessary, re-open the home.htm file worked on in previous exercise by double-clicking its entry in the Files panel.

4   In the CSS Styles panel, click Attach Style Sheet. When the Attach External Style Sheet dialog box opens, click Browse. In the Select Style Sheet File dialog box, navigate to the lesson03 > css folder and select print.css. Click OK (Windows) or Choose (MacOS) when you're done.

5   In the Attach External Style Sheet dialog box, verify that the Add as: Link option is selected. From the Media list, choose print and click OK.

As you can see in the CSS Styles panel, a new entry—print.css—has been added.

6   Choose File > Save.

Hiding unwanted page areas

By default, the Dreamweaver's Document window renders the browser page for the screen. However, Dreamweaver has the capacity to switch mediums through the Style Rendering toolbar. Once you've told Dreamweaver to display the print view of a page, you can quickly choose which styled areas are inappropriate for print and should be hidden.

1   If necessary, re-open the home.htm file worked on in previous exercise by double-clicking its entry in the Files panel.

2   Choose View > Toolbars > Style Rendering.

Alternatively, you can right-click (Windows) or Control+click (Mac) on the Insert bar and, from the pop-up menu, select Style Rendering.

3   From the Style Rendering toolbar, click Print (🖨).

One of the main differences between screen and print mediums is the lack of hyperlinks in print: therefore, the first task in the conversion of the style sheet is to hide any navigation elements.

4   Place your cursor anywhere in the main navigation below the logo and, from the Tag Selector, choose <div #nav>.

A hash mark (#) designates another type of custom selector called an ID. The primary difference between IDs and classes are that an ID may only be applied to one tag on the page whereas classes can be applied as many times as needed.

5   In the CSS Styles panel, click Current to enter Current mode.

In this situation, you'll see that there is no defined rule for #nav, so you'll need to create one that expressly hides the style's content.

6   From the CSS Styles panel, click New CSS Rule. When the New CSS Rule dialog box opens, choose Selector Type: Advanced and, in the Name field, enter **#nav**. From the Define in list, choose print.css and click OK.

7   When the CSS Rule Definition for #nav in print.css dialog box opens, click Block in the Category list. From the Display list, choose none and click OK.

Notice that the navigation is now hidden in the Document window. Now, let's take a look at how you modify an existing rule to not print.

8   Place your cursor in either of the two paragraphs with the .more class applied at the bottom of the document and, from the Tag Selector, choose <p .more>.

Because the CSS Styles panel is in Current mode, the .more rule is automatically selected.

9   In the Properties pane of the CSS Styles panel, click Add Property. In the first column, enter **display** and press Tab. From the list in the second column, choose none.

The page elements styled with the .more rule are now hidden from view.

10   Choose File > Save All.

Converting styles for print

Now that you've hidden parts of the Web page not appropriate for print, you're ready to adapt other styles to make them easier to read on a printed page.

1   If necessary, re-open the home.htm file worked on in previous exercise by double-clicking its entry in the Files panel.

2   In the CSS Styles panel, click All to switch to All mode.

3   Click the plus sign (Windows) or triangle (MacOS) to expand the print.css entry.

4   From the top of the All Rules list, choose body and then click Edit Style (✏️).

5   When the CSS Rule Definition for body in print.css dialog box opens, click Type in the Category list.

6   In the Type category, change the Size value from 76 to **100**. Click the Color swatch and, from the pop-up color picker select any black color swatch with the eyedropper tool. Click OK when you're done.

The general font for the <body> tag is increased to a standard 100% size and changed to the color with the highest contrast, black. Next, you'll change the page from a two column to a single column format.

7   From the CSS Styles panel All Rules list, choose #leftColumn. In the Properties pane, click the value next to the float property and choose none from the list. Select the width property and press Delete (Windows) or forward delete (MacOS) to remove it.

The float property is used in CSS to move a section of the page out of the normal document flow and position it to the left or right of other content. By setting the float property to none, you're allowing the content to expand to its full width—which, by removing the width property, becomes 100% of the page. The last task is to apply the same changes to the other column.

8   From the All Rules list, choose #rightColumn. In the Properties pane, click the value next to the float property and choose none from the list. Select the width property and press Delete to remove it.

9   Choose File > Save All.

The print style sheet is now complete. To see the changes between the screen and print style sheets, use the Styles Rendering toolbar.

10   In the Style Rendering toolbar, choose Screen (▤).

Note: Another way to test your print style sheet is to preview the page in the browser and then choose File > Print or, if no printer is available, File > Print Preview (Windows) or File > Print and then choose Print (MacOS).

11   Choose File > Close All.

Congratulations, you've completed this lesson!

Review

▶ ## Review questions

1   What are the two types of sites used in Dreamweaver and what are their differences? What are their similarities?

2   How do you attach an external style sheet to a Web page?

3   True or False: You can only create styles for existing HTML tags on the current Web page.

4   What are two ways to apply a CSS class to a tag?

5   What are two ways to change the value of a CSS property?

6   What CSS property and value are used to hide any content associated with a CSS style?

▶ ## Review answers

1   Dreamweaver relies on a local and a remote site. The local site is a folder that resides on the designer's own computer system while the remote site is a folder found on the Internet host's computer. Both sites share the same folder structure and files.

2   From the CSS Styles panel, choose Attach Style Sheet. In the Attach External Style Sheet dialog box, choose the desired CSS file and select the media type.

3   False. In addition to creating CSS styles for HTML tags, you can also create custom styles. Moreover, a tag does not have to exist on the current page in order to define a style for it.

4   One method of applying a CSS class to a tag is to select the tag and then choose the style from the Property inspector's Style list. Another is to right-click (Windows) or Control+click (MacOS) on the tag in the Tag Selector and choose the style from the Set Class list in the pop-up menu.

5   Change a CSS property either through the Properties pane of the CSS Styles panel or through the Edit Style button, also located on the CSS Styles panel.

6   Use the display property set to none to hide any CSS styled content.

dev/design

Maya Ren: Creative Director

Unconventional resume

Art influences:	Gauguin, Czanne and Monet
Last book read:	The Terror by Dan Simmons
Favorite quote:	"Twenty years from now you will be more disappointed by the things that you didn't do than by the ones you did do. So throw off the bowlines. Sail away from the safe harbor. Catch the trade winds in your sails. Explore. Dream. Discover". – Mark Twain
Training:	Fine Arts degree from Cooper Union, New York City.
Place of birth:	Beaufort, South Carolina
Best memory:	Being tackled by my mother as I watched a hurricane blow a tree past our picture window.
Dream invention:	The replicator from Star Trek

Much of the Web designer's world revolves around text: entering, styling and updating all manner of words. T text tools in Dreamweaver are rich a varied. Enter headings and text with equal ease and quickly shift from one the other. Add a numbered or bullete list to stress key points. Bring in a tab data either manually or imported fro an external source. Whichever type o text element you choose, Dreamweav gives voice to your words.

4 Working with Text

In this lesson, you'll learn how to work with headings, paragraphs and other text elements in Dreamweaver and do the following:

- Enter heading and paragraph text.
- Include text from another source.
- Insert numbered and bulleted lists.
- Spell check your document.
- Search and replace text.
- Insert and modify tables.
- Import tabular data.

This lesson will take about 90 minutes to complete. Be sure you have copied Lessons/Lesson04 from the Adobe Dreamweaver CS3 Classroom in a Book CD to your hard drive before beginning. As you work on this lesson, you'll overwrite the start files. If you need to restore the start files, copy them again from the CD.

Previewing your completed file

To get a sense of the file you will work on in the first part of this lesson, let's preview the completed page in the browser.

1 Start Adobe Dreamweaver CS3.

2 If necessary, press F8 to open the Files panel and choose DW CIB from the site list.

3 In the Files panel, expand the lesson04 folder.

4 Select the spirit_final.htm file and press F12 (Windows) or Option+F12 (MacOS).

5 Preview the page in your primary browser.

Note the variety of text elements used: headings, paragraphs, lists and tables.

6 Close your browser and return to Dreamweaver.

Entering headlines and body text

Whenever you open a document in Dreamweaver, you're ready to enter or modify text. Dreamweaver makes it very easy to select the proper heading size and edit your text.

1 From the Files panel, double-click the lesson04 > spirit.htm file to open it.

The spirit.htm file is a largely unfinished Web page that mixes placeholder and final text.

2   Select the phrase below the main navigation bar, Placeholder heading, and press Delete (Windows) or forward delete (MacOS). Enter the phrase **Driven by imagination**. By default, text is initially entered unformatted. You can easily assign a basic format— such as an <h1>, <h2> or <p> tag—to any text block through the Property inspector.

3   If necessary, choose Window > Properties to display the Property inspector. With your cursor still in the newly-entered text, choose Heading 1 from the Format list.

Because an external style sheet is already attached to this Web page, the text takes on the assigned color, font, and size of the relevant CSS rule—all of which are displayed in the Property inspector.

In addition to the Format list, you can also use a keyboard shortcut to apply a basic format to text. Enter Ctrl+1 (Windows) or Cmd+1 (MacOS) to choose an <h1> format, Ctrl+2 (Windows) or Cmd+2 (MacOS) to choose an <h2> format, and so on, through <h6>. For the paragraph format use Ctrl+0 (Windows) or Cmd+0 (MacOS).

4   Place your cursor above the heading, Ahead of the curve, and enter the phrase **Our reality is visionary**. In the Property inspector, choose Heading 2 from the Format list.

5　With your cursor at the end of the just entered phrase, press Enter (Windows) or Return (MacOS). Enter the following paragraph:

We strive to move beyond the ordinary, every day. For us, the extraordinary is standard in whatever we do. Communicate your dreams to us and we'll bring them to life, more vivid than you ever thought possible.

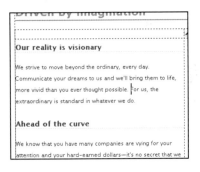

Note: You may have noticed that Dreamweaver automatically added a <p> tag following the <h2> tag. This action reflects the typical structure of Web page text and is optionally set in Preferences. If you'd prefer to insert a duplicate of the heading tag instead of a paragraph, choose Edit > Preferences and, in the General category, clear the Switch to plain paragraph after heading checkbox.

Once you've entered your text, you can manipulate it just as you would in any other quality text editor.

6　Select the second sentence in the paragraph just entered: **For us, the extraordinary is standard in whatever we do**. Be sure to include the space after the period. Drag it to the end of the paragraph after the phrase, **…ever thought possible**. Press Left+arrow to move your cursor to the beginning of the moved sentence and press the space bar.

So far, all of your work has been with a single tag, either an <h1>, <h2> or <p> tag. If you split a paragraph into two parts, Dreamweaver automatically creates the additional tag for you.

7   Place your cursor in the paragraph below the heading Ahead of the curve, in front of the second sentence that starts However, the dev/design crew and press Enter (Windows) or Return (MacOS).

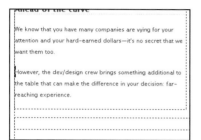

8   Choose File > Save.

The standard text editing tools—cut, copy and paste—are all available as well in Dreamweaver's Edit menu.

> *To separate text within a tag into two lines, press Shift+Enter (Windows) or Shift+Return (MacOS); this keyboard shortcut insert a line break or <br> tag. If you'd prefer to use the menus, choose Insert > HTML > Special Characters > Line Break.*

Importing external text

Although Dreamweaver provides excellent word processing support, designers often need to insert text created in an external application, like Microsoft Word. Dreamweaver offers a range of options for inserting text from an outside source, including copying and pasting, drag and drop, and linking. In this exercise, you'll insert a document created in Word by dragging it onto the page and selecting the proper option.

1   If necessary, re-open the spirit.htm file worked on in the previous exercise by double-clicking its entry in the Files panel.

2   Select the placeholder Placeholder paragraph in the column on the right side of the page and press Delete.

The inserted text will be added at the top of the column on the right.

3 In the Files panel, expand the lesson04 > assets folder.

Local Files	Size	Type	Modified	C
Site - DW CIB (C:\Project...		Folder	2/6/2007 8:03 PM	-
figs		Folder	2/19/2007 4:24 PM	-
lesson01		Folder	2/3/2007 2:36 PM	-
lesson02		Folder	2/11/2007 1:29 PM	-
lesson03		Folder	2/19/2007 6:30 PM	-
lesson04		Folder	2/19/2007 6:31 PM	-
assets		Folder	2/19/2007 3:27 PM	-
interview.csv	1KB	Microsoft Office Excel Comma ...	2/19/2007 3:27 PM	
Spirit_text.doc	24KB	Microsoft Word Document	2/17/2007 3:00 PM	
css		Folder	2/19/2007 4:25 PM	-
images		Folder	2/19/2007 2:39 PM	-
folks_maya.htm	9KB	Hypertext Markup Language	2/19/2007 6:30 PM	
folks_maya_final....	11KB	Hypertext Markup Language	2/19/2007 2:41 PM	
spirit_final.htm	11KB	Hypertext Markup Language	2/17/2007 10:19 PM	
spirit.htm	9KB	Hypertext Markup Language	2/17/2007 9:39 PM	
lesson05		Folder	2/3/2007 1:59 PM	-
lesson06		Folder	2/3/2007 1:59 PM	-

4 Drag the Spirit_text.doc file from the Files panel and drop in on the Web page in the current cursor position.

When you drop your dragged file, Dreamweaver recognizes the file as a Word document and opens the Insert Text dialog box. This dialog box presents a range of paste options from basic text to full formatting, along with an opportunity to insert a link to the external document.

Note: The above step is a Windows only operation. Macintosh users should open the document in Word and copy all the contents to the clipboard. Then, in Dreamweaver choose Edit > Paste Special and select the Text with structure plus basic formatting (bold, italic) option. Deselect "Clean up Word paragraph spacing" and click OK.

5   In the Insert Text dialog box, select the Insert the contents option and the Text with structure plus basic formatting (bold, italic) option. Click OK when you're done.

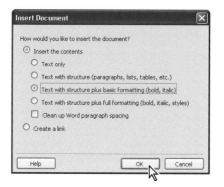

The Text with structure plus basic formatting option is chosen because the current Web page already has styles applied; if the Text with structure plus full formatting option were selected, the Word styles would be included and would need to be removed.

6   Choose File > Save.

Dreamweaver retains all of the paragraph breaks along with the italicized styling of the phrase esprit de corps; if you place your cursor within that phrase, you'll note that the Tag Selector indicates that the proper HTML <em> or emphasis tag is used. Dreamweaver automatically converts italics to <em> tags and bold to <strong> tags when inserting documents from external applications.

Note: You may notice a number of spelling errors in the inserted text. These errors are intentionally included and will be corrected later in this lesson.

Creating numbered and bulleted lists

Dreamweaver fully supports both numbered and bulleted lists. Each list item is contained on its own line and, if a numbered list is specified, automatically numbered. Bulleted lists have the option of using a built-in icon—such as a box or disc— or a specified image as the bullet symbol. In this exercise, you'll work with both numbered and bulleted lists.

Note: In HTML, a numbered list is designated with an <ol> or ordered list tag while a bulleted list uses a <ul> or unordered list tag.

1   If necessary, re-open the spirit.htm file worked on in the previous exercise by double-clicking its entry in the Files panel.

2   Select the four single-line paragraphs starting with Thorough pre-planning and ending with Realized return on investment.

3   From the Property inspector, click Ordered List (⅛≡).

Select the paragraphs you want to turn into a list.   Choose Ordered List for a numbered list.

4   Place your cursor in the third entry, Creative back-and-forth. From the Tag Selector, choose <li> and press Ctrl+X (Windows) or Cmd+X (MacOS) to cut the selection to the clipboard.

💡 *Alternatively, you could choose Edit > Cut from the Dreamweaver menu.*

Note that the list is renumbered automatically.

5   Press Up-arrow once to move your cursor in front of the second entry and press Ctrl+V (Windows) or Cmd+V (MacOS) to paste the clipboard contents.

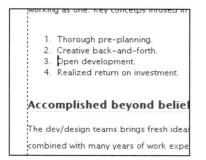

Dreamweaver makes it very simple to switch from one type of list to another.

6   From the Tag Selector, choose <ol>. In the Property inspector, click Unordered List (≡).

A CSS rule which increases the line height of the unordered list items has been previously added to the external style sheet attached to this page. In the next step, you'll add a new property to this rule to modify the bullet symbol.

7   Place your cursor in any of the list items of the bulleted list and choose Window > CSS Styles. In the CSS Styles panel, click Current to switch to Current mode. In the Rules panel, select ul li and click Edit Style. When the CSS Rule Definition for ul li in main.css dialog box opens, click List in the Category area. From the Type menu, choose disc and click OK.

8   Chose File > Save All to store changes both to the HTML and CSS files.

Spell checking your document

It's important to make sure the content you post to the Web is error-free. Dreamweaver includes a robust spell checker capable of identifying commonly misspelled words and creating a custom dictionary.

1   If necessary, re-open the spirit.htm file worked on in the previous exercise by double-clicking its entry in the Files panel.

2   Place your cursor in the <h1> heading, Driven by imagination, and press Ctrl+Home (Windows) or Cmd+Home (MacOS) to move the cursor to the top of the page.

Dreamweaver starts the spell check operation from the current cursor position and when it reaches the end of the document offers to start again from the top, if necessary. By positioning the cursor at the top of the document, this step is avoided.

3 Choose Text > Check Spelling.

When the Check Spelling dialog appears, it immediately flags the first error it encounters, the misspelled word motivete.

Check Spelling ☒

Word not found in dictionary:

motivete   <u>A</u>dd to Personal

Change <u>t</u>o: motivate

Suggestions: motivate
motivated
motivates
motive
emotive
motiveless
motivator
motives

<u>I</u>gnore

<u>C</u>hange

Ignore All

Change A<u>l</u>l

Close   <u>H</u>elp

4 With the first entry in the Suggestions list selected, motivate, click Change. After the next error is located, click Change to replace the word not found in the dictionary with the correct suggestion. Repeat this process until all incorrectly spelled words are replaced. When Dreamweaver notes that the spelling check is complete, click OK.

5 Choose File > Save.

If Dreamweaver identifies a properly spelled word as not found in the dictionary, you can choose Ignore for Dreamweaver to skip it or Add to Personal to insert the word into your personal dictionary. Dreamweaver compares words not found in the system dictionary to those stored in the personal dictionary and, if found, ignores it.

💡 *If none of the suggested words in the Check Spelling dialog box match the proper spelling of a word, you can enter the correctly spelled word in the Change to field manually and click Change.*

Searching and replacing text

The ability to find and replace text is one of Dreamweaver's most powerful features. Designers can target any amount of text, from a selection in the current document to the entire site. You can search just the rendered text on the page, the underlying tags or both simultaneously. Advanced users can enlist powerful pattern matching algorithms called regular expressions for the most sophisticated find and replace operations.

In this exercise, you'll find and replace a single phrase in the current document as an introduction to this feature.

1   If necessary, re-open the spirit.htm file worked on in the previous exercise by double-clicking its entry in the Files panel.

2   Choose Edit > Find and Replace. When the Find and Replace dialog box opens, from the Find in list, choose Current Document and from the Search list, choose Text.

💡 *You'd do well to take a moment to familiarize yourself with the options in both the Find in and Search lists. The Find in list controls the scope of the search; available options include selected text, current document, the open documents, a specified folder, documents chosen in the Files panel or the current site. The Search list determines the type of search: the source code, the text in Design view, text located within set code or specific tags.*

In this exercise, you'll search for the phrase dev/design and replace with the site specified phrase dev / design. The replacement phrase separates the two words with extra spaces on either side of the forward slash and replicates the look-and-feel of the site's logo.

3   In the Find field, enter the phrase **dev/design** and click Find Next.

Dreamweaver locates the first instance of the phrase.

With the Find Next option, you can examine each found instance and determine if it should be replaced.

4 In the Replace field, enter the phrase **dev / design** and click Replace.

Dreamweaver replaces the first instance of the found phrase and immediately searches for the next instance. To see all of the instances at once, choose Find All.

5 In the Find and Replace dialog box, click Find All. When the Results panel displays the found instances in the Search category, double click the second entry to locate it on the page.

Note: Unlike with most operations involving a dialog box, both the Find and Replace dialog box and the page itself are available for editing simultaneously.

When you're confident that Dreamweaver is replacing the proper phrase, you can use the Replace All option to find and replace all instances in the specified scope.

6 Click the green arrow on the side of the Search panel. In the Find and Replace dialog box, click Replace All.

After the Find and Replace operation is complete Dreamweaver automatically closes the dialog box. The results of the operation are displayed in the bottom of the Results panel. In this exercise, you should see: Done. 2 items found. 2 replaced in the current document.

💡 *A green dot next to an entry in the Results panel indicates that the instance was successfully replaced.*

▼ **Results**	Search	Reference	Validation	Browser Compatibility Check	Link Checker	Site Reports	FTP Log	Server Debug

File	Matched Text
[current document]	The dev / design teams brings fresh ideas and high energy combined with many years of work experience:
[current document]	© 2007 dev / design LLC.

Done. 2 items found, 2 replaced in the current document.

7   From the Results panel's Options menu, choose Close panel group. Choose File > Save.

Building tables

Tables are an effective tool for presenting structured data in a series of rows and columns. Dreamweaver provides a table object that is easily inserted and just as easily modified, both in Design view and through the Property inspector.

1   If necessary, re-open the spirit.htm file worked on in the previous exercise by double-clicking its entry in the Files panel.

2   Place your cursor on the line below the lower right column paragraph that starts The dev / design teams brings fresh ideas.

3   From the Insert bar's Common category, choose Table (⊞).

4   When the Table dialog box opens, in the Rows field, enter **4**. Press Tab and enter **2** in the Columns field. In the Table width field, enter **100**; press Tab and choose percent from the Table width list. Enter 0 in the Border thickness field and press Tab. Finally, choose Top from the Header area and click OK.

The specified table is inserted into the page at the current cursor location, ready for data or fine-tuning. Because the 100% width value was used, the table expands to fill the column.

Note: If you do not see the outline of the table cells, enable Table Borders from the Visual Aids menu on the Document toolbar.

5   In the first cell of the table (on the top row in the left column), enter **Team**. Press Tab and enter **Experience** in the top row, right column. Press Tab again to move to the second row.

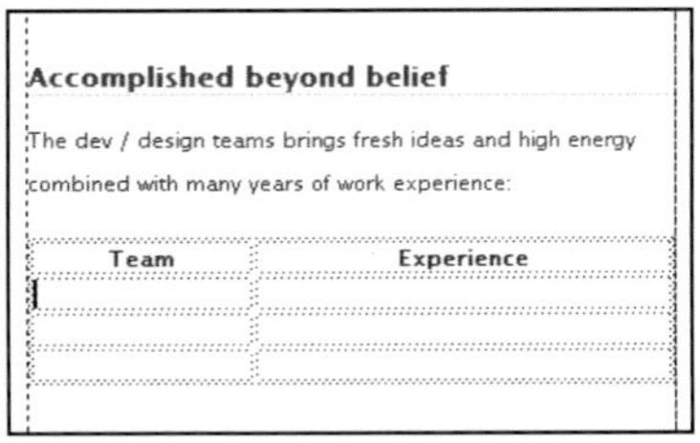

Because this row is designated as a header row, the entries are automatically bolded and centered; you'll have an opportunity to adjust the style later in this exercise.

The Tab key is the easiest way to move around a table; press Tab once to move to the next table cell to the right. If your cursor is in the last cell of the row, pressing Tab moves it to the first cell of the next row.

💡 *To go backwards in a table, press Shift+Tab.*

6   Enter the following text in the table, as shown below:

Graphics   **18 years**
Interactive   **27 years**
Copywriting   **23 years**

Often the number of rows and/or columns that initially defines a table needs to be modified. Dreamweaver offers a number of ways to make this change; let's add another row with one of the more flexible methods.

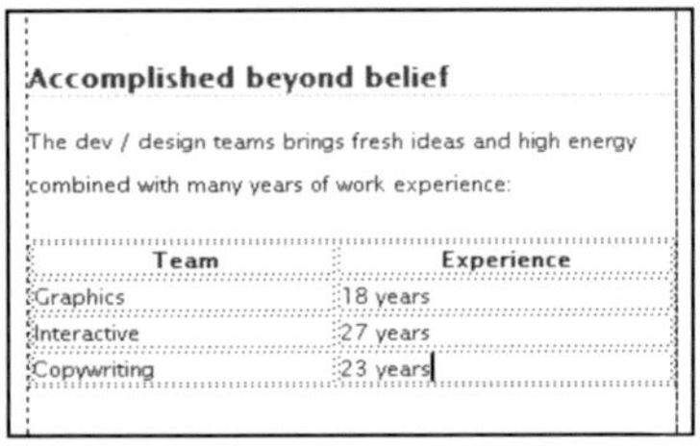

7   From the Tag Selector, choose <table>. In the Property inspector, change the Rows value from 4 to **5** and press Tab.

The new row is added to the bottom of the table. If you were to increase the number of columns, the new columns would be added to the right of the table.

> For complete control over where new table rows and columns are added, place your cursor in the cell adjacent to where you'd like your new rows or columns to appear and choose Modify > Table > Insert Rows or Columns.

8   In the new row, enter **Management** and press Tab. Enter **32 years** in the last table cell.

To follow HTML standard practices, Dreamweaver uses table header or <th> tags for any designed header cells—a practice that makes them easy to style.

9   If necessary, choose Window > CSS Styles. From the CSS Styles panel, choose New CSS Rule. In the New CSS Rule dialog box, select the Selector Type: Tag option and enter **th** in the Tag field. Make sure that the Define in: option is set to main.css and click OK.

10   When the CSS Rule Definition for th in main.css dialog box appears, click Block in the Category list. From the Text align list, choose left and click OK.

By default, browsers (and Dreamweaver) render <th> tags centered and bold. The new style rule shifts the alignment to the left, but maintains the bold format.

11   Choose File > Save and press F12 (Windows) or Option+F12 (MacOS) to preview the page in your primary browser. When you're done, close your browser and return to Dreamweaver and choose File > Close.

When previewed in the browser, the structure of the table is quite apparent, even though the table outlines are not visible.

Importing tabular data

In addition to working with text from word processing programs, Dreamweaver also has the capacity to incorporate tabular data from a spreadsheet or database program. To be imported into Dreamweaver, the data must be stored in a tab-delimited or comma separated format. On import, the data is inserted into Dreamweaver in a table which can then be styled or otherwise modified.

1   In the Files panel, double-click the folks_maya.htm file to open it.

2   Place your cursor in the right-side column on the line underneath the heading Unconventional resume.

3   Choose File > Import > Tabular Data. In the Import Tabular Data dialog box, click the Browse button. When the Open dialog box appears, navigate to the lesson04 > assets folder and select the interview.csv file; click Open to confirm your choice and close the Open dialog box.

Note: *The file extension .csv is short for comma separated values, although the actual delimiter in the file may vary. In this case, a tab character is used to separate the data in each row.*

4   From the Delimiter list, choose Tab. Choose the Table width: Set to option and enter **100** in the associated field and select Percent from the list. In the Border field, enter **0**; click OK when you're done.

Dreamweaver inserts a table containing the tabular data on the page, ready for customization. The first column is a bit narrow, so let's widen it to fix all the entries on a single line.

5   Place your cursor in the first cell of the inserted table which contains the phrase Art influences. If necessary, choose Window > Properties to display the Property inspector. In the W (for Width) field, enter **35%** and press Tab.

The top cell of any column controls the width for the column; you could have also modified the width by dragging the column border to a new position. Now, let's apply a style to all the cells in the column.

6   With your mouse in the first cell of the left column, drag your mouse down the entire column to select all of the cells. In the Property inspector, choose interviewHeader from the Style list. Click anywhere on the page to clear the selection.

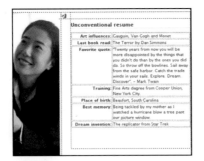

The interviewHeader style makes the text bold, right-aligned and vertically aligned to the top.

7   Choose File > Save and press F12 (Windows) or Option+F12 (MacOS) to preview the page in your primary browser. When you're done, close your browser and return to Dreamweaver and choose File > Close.

Congratulations, you've completed this lesson!

Review

▶ Review questions

1 True or False: Each heading and paragraph must be individually styled to appear differently in Dreamweaver.

2 What happens when you drag a Microsoft Word document onto a Dreamweaver page on a Windows system?

3 True or False: Once you've added a numbered list to the page, the only way to convert it to a bulleted list is to cut and re-insert it.

4 What kinds of search and replace operations are available in Dreamweaver?

5 What are two ways to change the number of rows or columns in a Dreamweaver table?

▶ Review answers

1 False. Dreamweaver allows designers to use the Property inspector to assign <h1> through <h6> tags for headings and <p> tags for paragraphs.

2 Dreamweaver opens the Insert Document dialog box and presents you with a series of options for including the text. The options include inserting the text in a variety of ways—from simple to fully formatted and styled—or inserting a link to the document.

3 False: To change a numbered list to a bulleted list, choose the numbered or ordered list tag in the Tag Selector, <ol>, and, from the Tag Selector, click Unordered List.

4 Dreamweaver can search the text in Design view, the underlying code or both. The scope of the search can range from a block of selected text, to the current page, to a folder of pages, to the entire site.

5 To modify the number of rows or columns in a Dreamweaver table, you can either a) select the table and then change the Rows or Cols values in the Property inspector or b) place your cursor next to the row or column you want to add and choose Modify > Table > Insert Rows or Columns.

dev/design

Home   Spirit   Folks   Work   Contact

Ready to move

Bringing light to the dark

Lorem ipsum dolor sit amet, consetetur sadipscing elitr, sed diam nonumy eirmod tempor invidunt ut labore et dolore magna aliquyam erat, sed diam voluptua. At vero eos et accusam et justo duo dolores et ea rebum. Stet clita kasd gubergren, no sea takimata sanctus est Lorem ipsum dolor sit amet.

No cliches allowed

Lorem ipsum dolor sit amet, consetetur sadipscing elitr, sed diam nonumy eirmod tempor invidunt ut labore et dolore magna aliquyam erat, sed diam voluptua.

Learn more about our spirit »

Interactivity re-defined

Lorem ipsum dolor sit amet, consetetur sadipscing elitr, sed diam nonumy eirmod tempor invidunt ut labore et dolore magna aliquyam erat, sed diam voluptua. At vero eos et accusam et justo duo dolores et ea rebum. Stet clita kasd gubergren, no sea takimata sanctus est Lorem ipsum dolor sit amet.

Lorem ipsum dolor sit amet, consetetur sadipscing elitr, sed diam nonumy eirmod tempor invidunt ut labore et dolore magna aliquyam erat, sed diam voluptua. At vero eos et accusam et justo duo dolores et ea rebum. Stet clita kasd gubergren, no sea takimata sanctus est Lorem ipsum dolor sit amet

Penny saved = penny earned

At vero eos et accusam et justo duo dolores et ea rebum. Stet clita kasd gubergren, no sea takimata sanctus est Lorem ipsum dolor sit amet. Stet clita kasd gubergren, no sea takimata sanctus est Lorem ipsum dolor sit amet..

Learn more about our work »

There can be no doubt that the Web is a highly visual medium. Dreamweaver provides a great number of ways to work with graphics, both within the program itself and with other dedicated graphic authoring tools, including Adobe Fireworks CS3 and Adobe Photoshop CS3. Adobe Bridge CS3 ties all the applications together to give you the power to explore your visual dreams.

5 | Designing with Images

In this lesson, you'll learn how to include images in your Web pages by doing the following:

- Insert an image.

- Apply a background image.

- Optimize an incorporated image.

- Add Adobe Fireworks rollovers to a page.

- Import an Adobe Photoshop file.

- Copy and paste an image from Photoshop.

- Work with Adobe Bridge.

This lesson will take about 90 minutes to complete. Be sure you have copied Lessons/Lesson05 from the Adobe Dreamweaver CS3 Classroom in a Book CD to your hard drive before beginning. As you work on this lesson, you'll overwrite the start files. If you need to restore the start files, copy them again from the CD.

Previewing your completed file

To get a sense of the file you will work on in the first part of this lesson, let's preview the completed page in the browser.

1   Start Adobe Dreamweaver CS3.

2   If necessary, press F8 to open the Files panel and choose DW CIB from the site list.

3   In the Files panel, expand the lesson05 folder.

4   Select the images_final.htm file and press F12 (Windows) or Option+F12 (MacOS)..

5   Preview the page in your primary browser.

The page includes a number of images, both foreground and background, as well as Fireworks-generated rollovers in the navigation bar.

6   Close your browser and return to Dreamweaver.

Inserting an image

Images are a key component of any Web page. Dreamweaver makes it easy to insert Web graphics in a number of ways, as you'll learn in this exercise.

1   From the Files panel, expand the lesson05 folder and double-click the images_start. htm file to open it.

Placeholder images are used to indicate where some of the graphics will be inserted during this lesson.

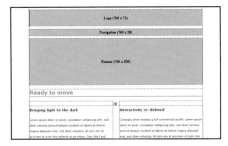

2   Select the Banner placeholder image and press Delete (Windows) or forward delete (MacOS).

3   From the Common category of the Insert bar, click Image (▥) .

If you don't see the Image icon in the Insert bar, click the down arrow next to the Images menu button and select Image. Like other menu buttons on the Insert bar, the Images menu button displays the object last chosen as the first entry.

4   When the Select Image Source dialog box appears, navigate to the lesson05 > images folder and select boat. Click OK when you're done.

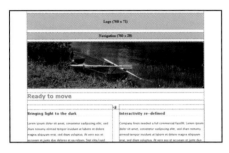

💡 *You can also double-click an image placeholder to open the Select Image Source dialog box and exchange the placeholder for an actual graphic.*

To make sure your pages are accessible to site visitors using screen readers or other assistive technologies, it's a good idea to always add appropriate alt text to any inserted image.

5   If necessary, choose Window > Properties to display the Property inspector.

6   With the boat image still selected, enter **Red rowboat by the side of a river** in the Alt field of the Property inspector and press Tab.

▼ Properties							
Image, 53K	W 760	Src images/boat.jpg		Alt Red rowboat by th
Banner	H 200	Link		Edit
Map	V Space	Target		Border
H Space	Low Src			Align Default

Another technique for adding an image to the page is to use the Assets panel.

7 Choose Window > Assets. When the Assets panel opens, click the Images category (⊞), the top icon in the column on the left of the panel. Scroll down to locate and select the streetlights.jpg image.

8 Drag the image preview from the Assets panel to the Document window and drop it in front of the first paragraph of the left column below the heading that reads Bringing light to the dark.

Alternatively, you could place your cursor in front of the paragraph and, with streetlights.jpg selected, click Insert at the bottom of the Assets panel.

9 In the Alt field of the Property inspector, enter **Streetlights along a road at night**.

10 Choose File > Save.

Using image placeholders

Image placeholders are a great tool for developing Web pages when the final images are not available. As you have seen in the starting points for various lessons in this book, including this one, an image placeholder is rendered in Dreamweaver as a plain rectangle with a title and the dimensions of the intended image. Image placeholders are intended for design-time only; if the page is previewed in a browser, the image placeholders do not appear, although some browsers—such as Internet Explorer—indicate a missing figure. To insert an image placeholder, follow these steps:

1 Place your cursor where you'd like the image placeholder to appear.

2 In the Common category of the Insert bar, select Image Placeholder ( ) from the Images menu button.

3 When the Image Placeholder dialog box opens, enter the name of the object in the Name field. Your entry will appear in the rendered image placeholder, along with the dimensions.

Note: *The name should not include spaces or special characters. Mixed case names, like ourHouse, or names with underscores (i.e., Our_House) are permitted.*

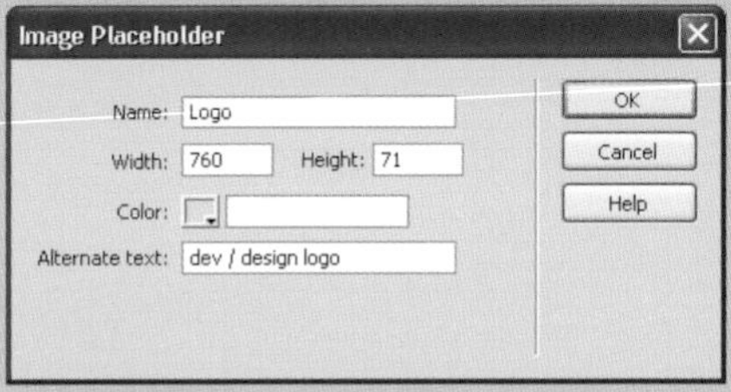

4 Enter the desired width in the Width field and height in the Height field.

Once inserted, the image placeholder can also be resized in Design view at any time.

5 If you'd prefer a different color from the default gray, click the Color swatch to open the color picker.

6 Enter the alt text for the intended image in the Alternative text field and click OK when you're done.

To replace the placeholder image with an actual graphic, double-click the placeholder image and choose your desired image from the Select Image Source dialog box. Both the name and alt text attribute values will be carried over from the image placeholder to the newly inserted image.

Using background images

Web pages can incorporate two different types of images: foreground and background. Foreground images are Web graphics (JPG, GIF, or PNG format) that are added to the document as an <img> tag; the previous exercise inserted two foreground images. Background images, on the other hand, are included in the page through CSS.

1   If necessary, re-open the images_start.htm file worked on in the previous exercise by double-clicking its entry in the Files panel.

2   Select the logo image placeholder and press Delete (Windows) or forward delete (MacOS) to remove it.

3   Choose Window > CSS Styles and, if necessary, click All to enter All mode.

4   In the main.css listing, choose #logo and click Edit Style (✐).

5   When the CSS Rule Definition for #logo in main.css dialog box opens, click Background in the Category list.

6   Click Browse and, in the Select Image Source dialog box, navigate to the lesson05 > images folder and select logo.gif.

7 From the Repeat list, choose no-repeat and click OK.

CSS Rule Definition for #logo in main.css

Category	Background
Type
Background	Background color:
Block
Box	Background image: ../images/logo.gif Browse...
Border
List	Repeat: no-repeal
Positioning	Attachment:
Extensions	Horizontal position: pixels
	Vertical position: pixels

Help   OK   Cancel   Apply

By default, background images tile, both horizontally and vertically to fill the container space. To display an image once, as is desired here, you must specify the no-repeat value.

8 Choose File > Save All.

Because the #logo CSS style rule is stored in an external style sheet, Dreamweaver automatically opens the file to change the style. Both the main document and the style sheet must be saved to store the current document look-and-feel.

Optimizing graphics

The optimum Web graphic balances image clarity with file size. It is not uncommon for the Web designer to need to optimize graphics that have already been placed on the page. Dreamweaver includes a graphics engine that is perfect for getting the best image at the lowest possible file size. In this exercise, you'll use Dreamweaver's built-in tools to optimize an image for the Web as well as rescale the graphic, another common design-time task.

1 If necessary, re-open the images_start.htm file worked on in the previous exercise by double-clicking its entry in the Files panel.

2 Place your cursor in front of the second paragraph of the right-side column, before the placeholder phrase Lorem ipsum dolor sit amet.

3 From the Common category of the Insert bar, choose Image from the Images menu button.

4 When the Select Image Source dialog box opens, navigate to the lesson05 > images folder and choose gears.jpg. Click OK when you're done.

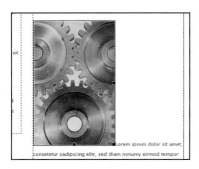

Not only is this graphic too big for the column area, at 103K it's also quite large in file size. Before rescaling to a more page-appropriate size—and a more Web-friendly file size—let's align the image to the right with a pre-defined CSS class.

5   If necessary, choose Window > Properties to display the Property inspector. With the inserted image selected, choose imageRight from the Class list.

Images can be easily resized by dragging any of the three sizing handles found on a selected graphic. Images resized in Dreamweaver by this technique are not actually rescaled, but merely re-rendered with different dimensions. You can, however, use Dreamweaver's resizing ability to visually establish the desired size—which is then automatically applied by the Optimize command.

A selected image has 3 sizing handles.

6   Begin to drag the sizing handle on the lower-right corner of the image to the upper-left; while you are dragging, press and hold the Shift key to maintain the original width/ height ratio. When you've reduced the image to approximately 2/3 the original size, release your mouse first, then release the Shift key. If you had the Property inspector open in the previous step, your image's new width should be 125 and height 188.

> *For a more precise resizing, make sure the Property inspector is open—both the width and height fields change dynamically as you resize the image.*

Now that the graphic fits better visually into the page, let's optimize it to lower the file size and simultaneously resample the image for the new smaller size.

7   With the image selected, click Optimize (🖸) in the Property inspector. When the Image Preview dialog box opens, make sure JPEG is chosen from the Format list. Click and drag the Quality slider to 80.

The Image Preview dialog box offers many different image optimization options, including the ability to switch from one Web graphic format, like GIF, to another, such as JPEG. With the JPEG format, you can also control the degree of quality: the higher the quality, the more detailed the image and the greater the file size. Let's use the comparison feature to find the optimal balance of clarity and size.

8   In the lower right area of the Image Preview dialog box, click 2 preview windows (▭). When the preview splits into two views, click the bottom view and drag the Quality slider to 50.

As you can see, there's a noticeable difference in image quality between the two previews. The file sizes differences—10.56K for the JPEG at 80 and 5.40K for the 50— while not huge, are still significant. At 50, the image quality has degraded visibily. Let's try a slightly higher quality setting for a better balance.

Note: You might notice that the much larger file size shown in the Property inspector (103K) has been largely reduced... The substantial reduction is attributable to the automatic rescaling applied when the Image Preview dialog box opened, as described in the next step.

9 Make sure you still have the lower preview area selected and drag the Quality slider to 65. If the image quality seems appropriate, click the File tab. Note that the Scale values (percentage and dimensions) have already been set: the Image Preview dialog box picks up whatever resizing has been applied in the Document window. Click OK to accept all the new image settings.

10 If the Save Web Image dialog box opens, navigate to the lesson05 > images folder and click OK. When Dreamweaver asks if you'd like to overwrite the existing file, click Yes (Windows) or Replace (MacOS).

The rescaled, optimized image is inserted into the page, lowering the file weight of the overall page significantly while maintaining a highly appealing, visual appearance.

11 Choose File > Save to store your work.

Additional built-in graphic tools

In addition to the optimizing tool discussed in this exercise, Dreamweaver offers a number of other useful image manipulation functions. All of Dreamweaver's graphic tools are accessible from the Property inspector, once an image has been selected. The six functions are:

A. Edit B. Optimize C. Crop
D. Resample E. Brightness
and Contrast F. Sharpen

• *Edit ( )- Sends the selected image to the defined external graphic editor. You can choose the program you'd like to assign to any given file type through the File Types / Editors category of Preferences. The tool button image changes according to the program chosen: if Fireworks is the designated editor for the image type, a Fireworks icon is shown; if Photoshop is the editor, you'll see a Photoshop icon.*

• *Optimize ( )- Opens the current image in the Image Preview dialog box. In addition to the optimization features noted in this exercise, the Image Preview dialog box can also be used to crop images and even modify animated GIF settings.*

• *Crop ( )– Cuts off the unwanted part of an image. When the Crop tool is selected, a bounding box appears within the current image with a series of handles. Adjust the bounding box by dragging the handles; when the box outlines the desired portion of the image, double-click the graphic to complete the operation.*

• *Resample ( )– Rescales a resized image. The Resample tool only becomes active when an image has been resized.*

• *Brightness and Contrast ( )– Adjusts an image that may be too light or too dark. A dialog box presents two sliders—one for brightness and the other for contrast—that can be adjusted independently. A live preview is available so you can see the effects before committing to them.*

• *Sharpen ( )– Affects the definition of the edges within the image by raising or lowering the contrast of the pixels on a sliding scale from 0 to 10. As with the Brightness and Contrast tool, Sharpen offers a real-time preview.*

All graphic operations, except Edit and Optimize, can be reversed by choosing Edit > Undo, until the containing document is closed or you quit Dreamweaver.

Including Fireworks rollovers

Navigation bars are common Web page elements comprised of a series of sliced graphical images and links in a single unified structure. The containing structure is often an HTML table. With Fireworks, you can create the entire navigation bar in a graphical environment—complete with links—and easily import it into Dreamweaver in a single operation.

Note: This exercise requires Adobe Fireworks CS3.

1   Start Adobe Fireworks CS3.

2   Choose File > Open. When the Open dialog box appears, navigate to the lesson05 > source folder and select navbar.png. Click Open.

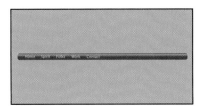

The complete navigation bar is ready for export.

💡 *Although creating navigation bars or other graphics in Fireworks is beyond the scope of this book, feel free to explore the structure of the navbar.png file. By examining the Layers panel, you'll find that it consists of a rectangle and five sliced button symbols, one for each navigation link.*

3   Choose File > Export. When the Export dialog box opens, navigate to the lesson05 > images folder.
The key to successfully exporting a sliced graphic from Fireworks for import in Dreamweaver is to export both the HTML and images; Fireworks has a setting for just this purpose.

4   Leave the default entry, navbar, in the File name field and make sure that HTML and Images is chosen from the Export list. From the HTML list, choose Export HTML File and, from the Slices list, choose Export Slices. Choose the Include areas without slices option, the Current page only option and the Put images in subfolder option.

Because slicing a graphic can result in a great deal of similarly named images, it's a good idea to keep all of the sliced images in their own subfolder. For example, the export of the navbar.png file results in 25 separate images. By default, Fireworks suggests the folder name images; to avoid confusion, let's give the folder a more specific name.

5 Click Browse (Windows) or New Folder (MacOS) to select a new subfolder. When the Select Folder dialog box opens, navigate to the lesson05 > images > navbar folder and click Save "navbar" (Windows) or Choose (MacOS). Once you've returned to the Export dialog box, click Save (Windows) or Export (MacOS).

6 After the operation is complete, choose File > Save and close Fireworks.

The export operation is deceptively quick. From a single graphic, Fireworks created an HTML file with all the sliced images in a single HTML table, complete with spacer images for cross-browser compatibility. Additionally, each of the individual graphics is saved in the subfolder, for both standard and rollover states.

7 If necessary, start Adobe Dreamweaver CS3.

8   From the Files panel, navigate to the lesson05 folder and re-open the images_start. htm file previously worked on in this lesson.

9   Select the placeholder image Navigation and press Delete (Windows) or forward delete (MacOS).

10   In the Common category of the Insert bar, choose Fireworks HTML (🖼) from the Images menu button.

11   When the Insert Fireworks HTML dialog box, click Browse to open the Select the Fireworks HTML file dialog box. Navigate to the lesson05 > images folder and select navbar.htm; click Open to confirm your choice. When the Insert Fireworks HTML dialog box reappears, leave the Delete file after insertion option unchecked and click OK.

Dreamweaver reads the code from the Fireworks HTML file and inserts just the required table structure. Additionally, the referenced graphics are preloaded to prevent the page from displaying without all of the images available.

12   Choose File > Save and then File > Close.

If you have the Property inspector open, you'll notice that when the table containing the Fireworks HTML is selected, the selection is designated as a Fireworks Table. In addition to the normal table options, you'll also see a Src attribute that lists the source PNG file. Click Edit to launch Fireworks, simultaneously opening the graphics source to make any necessary changes, including altering navigation button labels or changing the number of navigation buttons.

Inserting Photoshop files

As part of Adobe Creative Suite 3, Dreamweaver works seamlessly with other programs in the bundle, including Photoshop. There are numerous ways to move an image from one program to the other: one of the most straightforward is simply to open a native Photoshop PSD file in Dreamweaver. As a source file, Photoshop PSD files are not intended for the Web. However, when a PSD file is selected, Dreamweaver automatically presents the Image Preview dialog box, noted earlier in this chapter, to create a Web-ready graphic.

Note: The following exercise requires Adobe Photoshop CS3.

1   From the Files panel, navigate to the lesson05 folder and double-click the ps_bridge_start.htm file to open it.

2   Place your cursor before the first paragraph in the left column that starts We strive to move beyond the ordinary.

3   In the Common category of the Insert bar, click Image from the Images menu button.

4   When the Select Image Source dialog box opens, navigate to the lesson05 > source folder and select our_world.psd; click OK when you're ready.

5   When the Image Preview dialog box is displayed, drag the Quality slider to 60 and click the File tab. In the Scale area, make sure the Constrain option is selected and enter **360** in the Width field. When you're done, click OK.

Dreamweaver rescales the image and converts the PSD to a JPEG at the specified quality setting. Next, you'll get an opportunity to save the converted file in your site.

6   In the Save Web Image dialog box, navigate to the lesson 05 > images folder. Make sure that the File name field entry is our_world.jpg and click Save.

The newly-saved graphic is automatically inserted into the document at the current cursor position.

7   Choose File > Save.

Again, when the figure is selected, the Property inspector notes its special circumstances and presents a Photoshop source location as well as Photoshop edit button.

To modify a Photoshop image inserted into Dreamweaver, click the Edit Photoshop icon. When the graphic opens in Photoshop, make any necessary changes and then select all. Choose Edit > Copy Merged and return to Dreamweaver. Choose Edit > Paste to replace the current Web ready file with the revised one.

Copying and pasting from Photoshop

Many Web designers use Photoshop to initially compose (or comp) their site layouts. To create the actual Dreamweaver layout, only portions of the Photoshop graphic are needed; other page elements are text or CSS based. With Photoshop CS3 and Dreamweaver CS3, it's easy to copy any needed selection in from the graphic comp in Photoshop and paste it into the Dreamweaver layout. Again, the Image Preview dialog box acts as the intermediary to convert the file to the necessary format.

Note: *The following exercise requires Adobe Photoshop CS3.*

1   If necessary, re-open the ps_bridge_start.htm file worked on in the previous exercise by double-clicking its entry in the Files panel.

2   Place your cursor before the start of the paragraph in the right-side column that starts We want you involved in your re-design.

3   Start Adobe Photoshop CS3 and choose File > Open. When the Open dialog box appears, navigate to the lesson05 > source folder and select company_history.psd. Click Open.

The file opened is a comp for a different website. In this exercise, you'll select a portion of a photo to use in Dreamweaver.

4   From the Tools palette, select the Zoom tool and drag a rectangle around the photo on the right side of the comp. Next select the Rectangular Marquee tool and drag a selection within the purple border that encompasses the two pairs of legs on the left.

5   Choose Edit > Copy. Close Photoshop without saving the image and return to Dreamweaver.

If your selection included elements on more than one layer, you would need to choose Edit > Copy Merged.

6   In Dreamweaver, choose Edit > Paste. When the Image Preview dialog box opens, make sure that JPEG – Better Quality is chosen from the Saved Settings list and click OK.

7   When the Save Web Image dialog box opens, navigate to the lesson 05 > images folder. In the File name field, enter **jump.jpg** and click Save.

The image copied from Photoshop is inserted into the document. Let's float it to the right using a pre-defined CSS class.

8 Select the newly inserted image and, if necessary choose Window > Properties. In the Property inspector, choose imageRight from the Class list.

9 Choose File > Save.

Modifying portions copied from a Photoshop image is similar to altering inserted (and converted) Photoshop files. With the image selected, click Edit Photoshop from the Property inspector. When the image appears in Photoshop, make any desired corrections, copy the desired portion of the image and return to Dreamweaver to paste it in. Dreamweaver automatically applies the settings previously established in the Image Preview dialog box.

Accessing Bridge

Adobe Bridge CS3 is an aptly named program that acts as a common library for other Creative Suite application, including Dreamweaver. With Bridge, you can quickly browse directories of images and other supported assets, tag files with keywords, and easily access professional stock images sites, like Adobe Stock Photos. Bridge is fully integrated with Dreamweaver: you can launch Bridge from within Dreamweaver, drag and drop images from Bridge onto your Web pages or even place images directly into Dreamweaver, without ever leaving Bridge.

1 If necessary, re-open the ps_bridge_start.htm file worked on in the previous exercise by double-clicking its entry in the Files panel.

2 Place your cursor at the end of the paragraph in the left column, following the sentence that ends far-reaching experience. Press Enter (Windows) or Return (MacOS) to create a new line.

Later in this exercise, you'll place an image into Dreamweaver from Bridge at the current cursor location.

3 Choose File > Browse in Bridge.

4 When Bridge opens, click the Folders tab and navigate to the lesson05 > source folder and select cans.jpg.

5 Choose File > Place > In Dreamweaver.

Bridge inserts the file into Dreamweaver and brings Dreamweaver to the front. You can also drag images directly from Bridge into Dreamweaver; let's replace the last image with one that is more appropriate.

Note: If the source for the images placed or dragged from Bridge was outside the current Dreamweaver site, you would be given the opportunity to copy the file to your site.

6 Select the just-inserted image and press Delete (Windows) or forward delete (MacOS). Return to Bridge and click Switch to Compact Mode (▤), the last icon on the right of the top row of controls. Alternatively, you could choose View > Compact Mode.

Compact mode reduces the size of the Bridge interface to about ¼ of the screen and, by default, always keeps the program on top of others for easy browsing and dragging.

7 Drag track.jpg from the Bridge into Dreamweaver in the same position as the previously inserted image, at the bottom of the column on the left side.

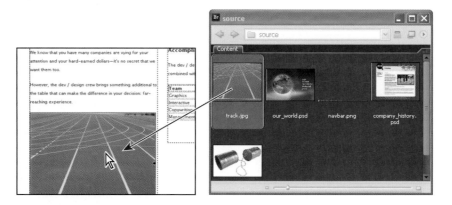

8 In Dreamweaver, choose File > Save. Press F12 (Windows) or Option+F12 (MacOS) to preview the page in your primary browser; be sure to roll over the navigation items to review the rollover effect. When you're done, return to Bridge and close the program.

Congratulations, you've completed this lesson!

Review

▶ **Review questions**

1   Describe two methods for inserting an image into a Web page in Dreamweaver.

2   True or False: Image placeholders can be used on the Web until you get your final images ready.

3   How do you insert a background image? What control do you have over such graphics.

4   True or False: All graphics have to be optimized outside of Dreamweaver.

5   Describe the process for adding a Fireworks created navigation bar to a Dreamweaver page.

6   What are two ways you can get images from Photoshop into Dreamweaver?

7   How is Adobe Bridge integrated into Dreamweaver?

▶ **Review answers**

1   One method is to choose Image from the Images menu button in the Common category of the Insert bar. and navigate to the graphic file you want to insert. Another method is to drag the graphic file from the Assets panel onto your page.

2   False. Image placeholders are a design-time tool only; browsers either completely omit the image placeholder or indicate an image not found.

3   CSS style rules are used to add a background image to a page element. Choose the selector of the element that will contain the background image, such as the <body> tag or a specific ID applied to a <div> tag and then add the appropriate background image properties. Background images, by default, tile to fill the containing space, but with CSS you can display the image only once or tile in either an X or Y direction.

4   False. Any image inserted into a Dreamweaver page can be optimized through the Image Preview dialog box. Optimization can include rescaling, change of format or fine-tuning of format settings.

5   Once a Fireworks graphic file has been exported with both HTML and sliced graphics, click the Insert Fireworks HTML object from the Images menu button on the Insert bar's Common category. In the resulting dialog box, browse for the exported HTML file and click OK. Dreamweaver does the rest.

6   You can open a native Photoshop PSD file or copy from Photoshop and paste in Dreamweaver. Both techniques use the Image Preview dialog box to convert the files to Web ready graphics.

7   Bridge can be opened from within Dreamweaver by choosing File > Browse in Bridge. Moreover, from within Bridge, you can choose File > Place > In Dreamweaver to insert a selected image into the current cursor position in Dreamweaver. Finally, images can be dragged directly from Bridge into Dreamweaver.

dev/design

Home   Spirit   Folks   Work   Contact

A few of our clients...

CarryAll Inc.

Lorem ipsum dolor sit amet, consetetur sadipscing elitr, sed diam nonumy eirmod tempor invidunt ut labore et dolore magna aliquyam erat, sed diam voluptua. At vero eos et accusam et justo duo dolores et ea rebum. Stet clita kasd gubergren, no sea takimata sanctus est Lorem ipsum dolor sit amet. Lorem ipsum dolor sit amet, consetetur sadipscing elitr, sed diam nonumy eirmod tempor invidunt ut labore et dolore magna aliquyam erat, sed diam voluptua. At vero eos et accusam et justo duo dolores et ea rebum. Stet clita kasd gubergren, no sea takimata sanctus est Lorem ipsum dolor sit amet.

Top »

Company Anon

Lorem ipsum dolor sit amet, consetetur sadipscing elitr, sed diam nonumy eirmod tempor invidunt ut labore et dolore magna aliquyam erat, sed diam voluptua. At vero eos et accusam et justo duo dolores et ea rebum. Stet clita kasd gubergren, no sea takimata sanctus est Lorem ipsum dolor sit amet. Lorem ipsum dolor sit amet, consetetur sadipscing elitr, sed diam nonumy eirmod tempor invidunt ut labore et dolore magna aliquyam erat, sed diam voluptua. At vero eos et accusam et justo duo dolores et ea rebum. Stet clita kasd gubergren, no sea takimata sanctus est Lorem ipsum dolor sit amet.

Top »

Lit City, LLC.

In some ways the Web is, at its heart, a collection of links. Within any given site, links provide a conduit to quickly navigate from one related topic to another. A link from one site to another can span vast distances with a single click. Links serve other functions as well, bringing up email messages for an interactive response or within an individual page to target a specific page area. Dreamweaver handles all of these link variations with straightforward ease and flexibility.

6 | Inserting Links

In this lesson, you'll learn how to apply different kinds of links to various page elements by doing the following:

- Apply a text link to a page within the same site.
- Link from an image.
- Create a link to a page on another website.
- Establish an email link.
- Link to a specific part of a page.

This lesson will take about 60 minutes to complete. Be sure you have copied Lessons/Lesson06 from the Adobe Dreamweaver CS3 Classroom in a Book CD to your hard drive before beginning. As you work on this lesson, you'll overwrite the start files. If you need to restore the start files, copy them again from the CD.

Previewing your completed file

To get a sense of the file you will work on in the first part of this lesson, let's preview the completed page in the browser.

1 Start Adobe Dreamweaver CS3.

2 If necessary, press F8 to open the Files panel and choose DW CIB from the site list.

3 In the Files panel, expand the lesson06 folder.

4 Select the links_final.htm file and press F12 (Windows) or Option+F12 (MacOS).

5 When the page opens in your primary browser, click the Spirit link in the main navigation; from the Spirit page, choose Back to return to links_final.htm. Click Maya Ren to visit another page; choose Back to return. If you have a mail client installed on your system, click the Got Something to Say? link at the bottom of the page. When the email form opens, close it.

The page includes a number of links to pages within the same site as well as external and email links.

6 Close your browser and return to Dreamweaver.

Linking to internal site pages

Links are a quintessential element of the Web and Dreamweaver makes it easy to apply them. In this exercise, you'll create both text and graphic links to other pages in the same site through a variety of methods.

1 From the Files panel, expand the lesson06 folder and double-click the links_start. htm file to open it.

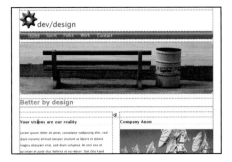

Although it may not be obvious from first glance, the current page does not include any complete links. Let's start by creating a few text links.

2   Place your cursor in the text at the bottom of the left side column that reads, Learn more about our spirit. From the Tag Selector, choose <p .more> to select the entire line.

3   If necessary, choose Window > Properties to open the Property inspector. Click Browse for File (🗀), the folder icon adjacent to the Link field. When the Select File dialog box opens, navigate to the lesson06 folder and select spirit.htm; click OK when you're done.

The text changes color because a CSS rule has been established that styles all links with a bright, bold orange. The Browse for Folder method provides a traditional technique for linking to files. Next, let's try a more visual approach.

4   In the paragraph following the heading Top dogs sleep here, select the words Maya Ren.

You can select any range of text to create a link; Dreamweaver will add the necessary tag around the selected text.

5   If necessary, press F8 to open the Files panel and expand the lesson06 folder.

6   From the Property inspector, drag Point to File (◎), the target icon next to the Link field to the Files panel and point to folks_maya.htm.

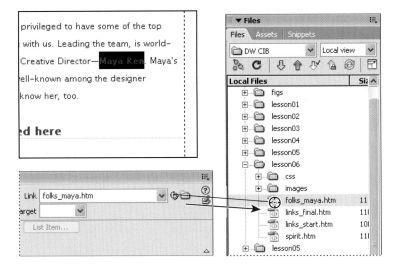

💡 *If a folder in the Files panel contains a page you want to link to, but is not open, drag the Point to File cursor over the folder to expand it so you can point to the desired file. Drag it over the folder again to close the folder.*

Either linking technique can be applied to graphic-based links.

7   In the main navigation bar, select the Spirit label. From the Property inspector, leave the placeholder link—javascript:; —in the Link field and drag the Point to File icon to spirit.htm in the Files panel folder lesson05.

Whenever you use either the Point to File or Browse for Folder method, the current link is replaced.

Note: The navigation bar, as seen in Lesson 04, was created in Adobe Fireworks CS3 and inserted into Dreamweaver. Fireworks temporarily uses the javascript:; code to trigger the rollover effect until links are added.

8   Choose File > Save.

Creating an external link

All of the pages linked in the previous exercise were within the current site. You can also link to any page on the Web, if you know the full Web address or URL.

1   If necessary, re-open the links_start.htm file worked on in the previous exercise by double-clicking its entry in the Files panel.

2   Select the image below the Company Anon heading.

3   In the Property inspector, enter the following into the Link field: **http://www.companyanon.com/** and press Tab.

If the Web address is too long or complex to type, browse to the desired page in your browser, and copy the URL from the Location field and then paste it into the Link field in Dreamweaver's Property inspector.

4   Choose File > Save and press F12 (Windows) or Option+F12 (MacOS) to preview the page in your primary browser. Note that when your cursor hovers over the image, it changes to a hand which indicates a link; if you click the image, the browser will not be able to display the page, as the company, and its website, are fictional. Close your browser and return to Dreamweaver.

Note: To conform to current HTML standards, Dreamweaver CS3 no longer automatically inserts a border="0" attribute in the <img> tag when a graphic link is created. To prevent all linked images from displaying a border, create a CSS rule like the following: img {border: 0;}.

Setting up email links

An email link, when clicked by the site visitor, opens a self-addressed email message. The code is different from the standard page link and uses a mailto: preface followed a valid email address. Dreamweaver can automatically create the proper code for any email link.

1   If necessary, re-open the links_start.htm file worked on in the previous exercise by double-clicking its entry in the Files panel.

2   Select the following text at the bottom of the page in the footer area: Got something to say?

uyam erat, sed diam voluptua. At vero eos et
t justo duo dolores et ea rebum. Stet clita kasd
no sea takimata sanctus est Lorem ipsum dolor sit

Got something to say? – © 2007 dev/design LLC.

3   From the Common category of the Insert bar, click Email Link (⊠), the envelope icon located second from the left.

4   When the Email Link dialog box appears, leave the current entry in the Text field and, in the E-mail field, enter **info@devdesign.com**. Click OK when you're done.

Email Link

Text: Got something to say?

E-Mail: info@devdesign.com

OK

Cancel

Help

There's no need to enter the mailto: preface; Dreamweaver handles the coding automatically.

5 Choose File > Save. If you have an email program installed on your computer, press F12 to preview the page in your browser and click the just-applied email link. After the email message appears, note that the To field is already addressed.

6 Close both the message and your browser and return to Dreamweaver.

Targeting links within the page

Typically, when you click a link to a page, the browser window displays the page from the top down. Certain designs, like very long pages, require a more targeted approach. With Dreamweaver, you can insert a named anchor anywhere on the page and link directly to that anchor. In this exercise, you'll insert a link from one page to a specific section in the middle of another page and also set named anchors to move from the middle to the top of the page.

1 If necessary, re-open the links_start.htm file worked on in the previous exercise by double-clicking its entry in the Files panel.

Let's start by adding some new text for our link.

2 Place your cursor at the bottom of the right side column, after the placeholder text Lorem ipsum dolor sit amet, and press Enter (Windows) or Return (MacOS) to create a new line.

3 Enter the following text: **Learn more about Company Anon**. Press Space and choose Insert > HTML > Special Characters > Other. When the Insert Other Character dialog box appears, choose the right angle quotation mark, on the second row, fourth from the right. Click OK.

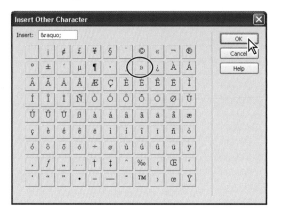

4 From the Tag Selector, choose <p>. In the Property inspector, select more from the Style list. With the tag still selected, enter the following in the link field: **work.htm#anon** and press Tab.

The hash mark (or number sign), #, designates an anchor link. The word following the hash mark—here, anon—is the name of the anchor link.

5 Choose File > Save and, from the Files panel, double-click the work.htm file to open it.

Your work in the links_start.htm file is now done, but you'll still need to insert the named anchor in the linked file.

6 Place your cursor in front of the Company Anon heading. From the Common category of the Insert bar, click Named Anchor (⚓), the anchor symbol third from the left.

7 When the Named Anchor dialog box opens, in the Anchor name field, enter **anon** and click OK.

Dreamweaver inserts an anchor symbol onto the page to designate where the code is placed. The connection from the previous page is now complete. However, to make it easier to work with lengthy pages, let's add another link and named anchor pair to move to the top of the page.

8 Place your cursor in the phrase Top » below the Company Anon paragraph and, from the Tag Selector, choose <p .more>. In the Link field of the Property inspector, enter **#top** and press Tab.

Because this link is to a named anchor in the same page, no file name is needed. The last step is to add the named anchor to the top of the page.

9 Place your cursor to the left of the dev / design logo and, from the Tag Selector, choose <div #wrapper>. Press left arrow to move before the selected <div> tag. From the Insert bar, click Named Anchor.

10 When the Named Anchor dialog box opens, in the Anchor name field, enter **top** and click OK.

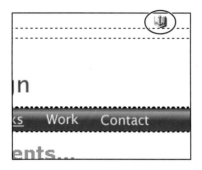

Again, the anchor symbol appears on the page to indicate the inserted code. Now you're ready to try out your named anchor links.

11 Chose File > Save and select the tab for links_start.htm. Press F12 (Windows) or Option+F12 (MacOS) to preview the page in your primary browser. Click the Learn more about Company Anon link. Note how the work.htm file opens with the Company Anon section at the top of the browser window. Click the Top » link to move to the top of the page.

12 When you're finished, close your browser and return to Dreamweaver. Choose File > Close All.

Congratulations, you've completed this lesson!

Review

1 Describe two ways to insert a link into a page.

2 True or False: You can only link to pages within a site in Dreamweaver.

3 What's the difference between standard page links and email links?

4 What two elements are necessary to establish a link within a page?

▶ **Review answers**

1 One technique is to select text or a graphic and then, in the Property inspector, select the Browse for File icon next to the Link field and navigate to the desired page. Another method is to drag the Point to File icon to a file within the Files panel.

2 False. Link to an external page by entering the full Web address (a fully formed URL) in the Link field of the Property inspector.

3 An email link uses the prefix, mailto: followed by a valid email address whereas a standard link uses a path to a file and the file name, like ../folks/rena_may.htm or http://www.companyanon.com/.

4 First, you'll need a named anchor placed where you'd like the page window to start; this can be inserted in Dreamweaver by clicking Named Anchor from the Common category of the Insert bar. Second, you'll need a link to that named anchor that uses the hash mark, #, and the name of the named anchor, for example, #top.

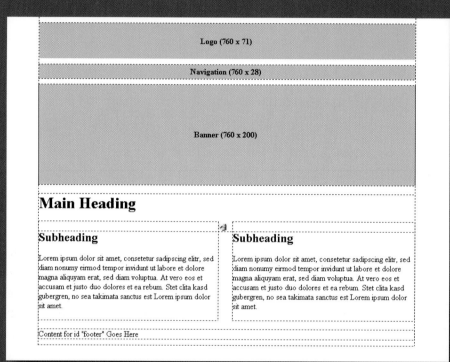

The Cascading Style Sheet (CSS) revolution continues to solidify its foothold in the Web designer community. Modern Web design techniques demand a structured, standards-compliant CSS-based layout—and Dreamweaver is happy to deliver. Dreamweaver renders CSS standards impeccably to help Web designers like yourself meet the challenges of building layouts through styles. Even better, Dreamweaver includes additional layout tools, such as rulers and guides, to help you shape your stylistic visions into real-world layouts.

7 | Crafting Page Layouts

In this lesson, you'll learn how to create and work with CSS-based page layouts by doing the following:

- Define the CSS rules for layout areas.
- Apply the CSS rules to inserted <div> tags.
- Add text and image placeholders to the page.
- Export the CSS rules to an external style sheet.
- Use rulers and guides to fine-tune a layout.

This lesson will take about 120 minutes to complete. Be sure you have copied Lessons/Lesson07 from the Adobe Dreamweaver CS3 Classroom in a Book CD to your hard drive before beginning. As you work on this lesson, you'll overwrite the start files. If you need to restore the start files, copy them again from the CD.

Previewing your completed file

To get a sense of the file you will work on in the first part of this lesson, let's preview the completed page in the browser.

1   Start Adobe Dreamweaver CS3.

2   If necessary, press F8 to open the Files panel and choose DW CIB from the site list.

3   In the Files panel, expand the lesson07 folder.

4 Double-click the layout_final.htm file to open it.

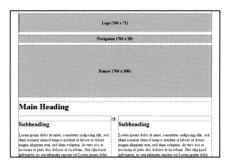

The page represents the basic layout used in the sample site, complete with a link to an external CSS file.

5 Choose File > Close.

Creating layout styled div elements

Best practices for today's Web designer require CSS-based layouts. A CSS-based layout—versus a table-based layout—reduces file size, is easier to manage and meets industry standards. Two basic components make up a CSS-based layout: a series of CSS rules that define the dimensions and format of key page elements and a corresponding series of HTML tags, typically <div> tags, that form the foundation of the page.

Creating the page and defining the body tag

In this exercise, you'll build a CSS-based layout from the ground-up—a blank HTML document. Once the file is created, you'll declare your first CSS rule for the <body> tag to make sure all browsers start from a level playing field.

1   Choose File > New. When the New Document dialog box opens, choose Blank Page. From the Page Type column, choose HTML and, from the Layout column, choose <none>. When you're ready, click Create.

If the Dreamweaver Welcome Screen is displayed, a quicker way to create a blank HTML page is to simply click the first entry under the Create New column, HTML.

2   Chose File > Save. In the Save As dialog box, navigate to the lesson07 folder and, in the File Name field, enter **layout_start.htm**. Click OK when you're done.

3   Choose Window > CSS Styles. When the CSS Styles panel opens, switch to All mode, if necessary, by clicking All.

4 From the bottom of the CSS Styles panel, click New CSS Rule (⊞).

It's a good idea to establish a neutral canvas for your layout by declaring a CSS rule for the <body> tag first.

5 When the New CSS Rule dialog box appears, choose Selector Type: Tag. In the Tag field, enter **body**. Select the Define in: This document only option and click OK.

Note: Although it's up to the individual designer, many Web professionals initially define their CSS layout rules in the <head> of the layout document. This practice simplifies development and eliminates the need to work with multiple files. After the design is complete, the rules are exported to an external style sheet, as described in an exercise later in this lesson.

6 In the CSS Rule Definition for body dialog box, click Background from the Category column. Click the Background color swatch to open the pop-up color picker and, with the Eyedropper tool, click the white swatch.

7 From the Category column, click Block. From the Text align list, choose center.

The layout under construction will be centered in the browser window, although the text will be aligned left. To render properly with older browsers, such as Internet Explorer 5.x, you need to first set the Text align property to center in the overarching <body> tag. A later CSS rule re-aligns the text to the left for items within a containing tag.

8   From the Category column, click Box. In the Padding area, enter **0** in the Top field. In the Margin area, repeat the action and enter **0** in the Top field. Click OK.

9   Choose File > Save.

Now, with the background color set to white and both the Padding and Margin properties at 0, your page is in a neutral state and you're ready to begin defining the layout containers for the page.

Defining the outer wrapper

A standard technique for creating a CSS-based layout is to employ a <div> tag that contains all other tags and content. The declaration of a single, outermost wrapper defines one rule for establishing global settings, such as overall width and layout alignment. In this exercise, you'll define the CSS rule and insert the associated <div> tag.

1   If necessary, re-open the layout_start.htm file worked on in the previous exercise by double-clicking its entry in the Files panel.

2   From the CSS Styles panel, click New CSS Rule.

3   When the New CSS Rule dialog box opens, choose Selector Type: Advanced. In the Selector field, enter **#wrapper**. Make sure the Define in: This document only option is selected and click OK.

You'll recall from Lesson 3 that the leading hash mark indicates an ID selector which can be applied once per page.

💡 *Dreamweaver remembers your settings from the last time you created a new CSS rule; many times you won't have to make changes to particular parameters.*

4   In the CSS Rule Definition for #wrapper dialog box, click Block in the Category column. From the Text align list, choose left.

In the previous exercise, the rule for the <body> tag sets the Text align property to center to maintain compatibility with older browsers. Because an ID selector like #wrapper has a higher specificity than the body tag selector, all elements eventually placed in the #wrapper <div> tag will be left-aligned and not centered.

5   From the Category column, click Box and, in the Width field, enter **760** and press Tab. In the Margin area, clear the Same for all checkbox. In the Top field, enter **0** and press Tab. From the Right list, choose auto. In the Bottom field, enter **0** and press Tab. From the Left list, choose auto. Click OK when you're done.

This layout design calls for a set width of 760 pixels, which works well for an 800 x 600 pixel screen size. Why not use a width of 800 pixels? The 40 extra pixels are used to display sides of the browser including any needed scroll bars; this area of the browser, along with sections above and below the main viewing window, are referred to as its chrome.

The left and right margins are set to auto in order to center the #wrapper <div> and, therefore, the contained page content. If the browser window is larger than the width—here, 760 pixels—the remaining width is divided and equally applied to the left and right margins, automatically. Now you're ready to insert the <div> tag within the #wrapper style. Dreamweaver offers a direct approach for handling both tasks at once.

6   From the Common category of the Insert bar, click Insert Div Tag (▦). When the Insert Div Tag dialog box opens, leave the Insert list at the default option, At insertion point. From the ID list, choose wrapper and click OK.

Dreamweaver adds the new <div> to the page, with the placeholder content that reads: Content for id "wrapper" Goes Here.

Note: If you don't see a dashed outline around the newly-inserted <div> tag, choose CSS Layout Outlines from the Visual Aids menu button on the Document toolbar.

7   Press F4 to close all panels and display the Document window fully. Notice that the outlined <div> tag, #wrapper, is centered in the Document window. Press F4 again to redisplay the panels and choose File > Save.

Now that the outer wrapper is in place, let's add the major layout divisions.

Setting up the primary divisions

The current design can be divided into three major areas: header, content section and footer. Each of these areas requires a separate CSS rule and <div> tag.

1   If necessary, re-open the layout_start.htm file worked on in the previous exercise by double-clicking its entry in the Files panel.

Let's define the first of our CSS rules, #header, to start.

2   In the CSS Styles panel, click New CSS Rule. When the New CSS Rule dialog box is displayed, enter **#header** in the Selector field. Verify that Selector Type: Advanced and Define In: This document only are chosen and click OK.

3   In the CSS Rule Definition for #header dialog box, click Box in the Category column. In the Margin area, uncheck the Same for all checkbox. In the Top field enter **12** and press Tab; in the Bottom field, enter **12** and press Tab again. Click OK.

When applied, the #header CSS rule will provide a little bit of space above and below the <div> tag. It's not necessary to declare a width because, by default, an HTML block element like a <div> tag expands to fill its container—which will be, in this case, the #wrapper <div> tag.

Let's continue and define the other two needed CSS rules.

4   In the CSS Styles panel, click New CSS Rule. When the New CSS Rule dialog box is displayed, enter **#content** in the Selector field. Verify that Selector Type: Advanced and Define In: This document only are chosen and click OK.

5   In the CSS Rule Definition for #content dialog box, click Box in the Category column. Clear the Same for All checkbox in the Padding area and, in the Top field, enter **0**. Uncheck the Same for all checkbox in the Margin area and enter **0** in the Top field. Click OK when you're done.

The final CSS rule to declare, #footer, is similar enough to the #header rule that you can take a short-cut to creating it.

6   In the CSS Styles panel, right-click (Windows) or Ctrl+click (MacOS) on the #header style and choose Duplicate from the pop-up menu. When the Duplicate CSS Rule dialog box is displayed, enter **#footer** in the Selector field and click OK.

When you duplicate an existing style rule, the new rule is inserted without the CSS Rule Definition dialog box appearing. If you need to make any adjustments, you can use the Properties pane of the CSS Styles panel.

7   In the CSS Styles panel, selector #footer and, from the Properties pane, click Add Property. In the first column, enter **clear** and press Tab. From the second column list, choose both.

Here, the clear: both CSS property ensures that no floated elements will intrude on the #footer. As you'll see later in this exercise, the content area will contain two floated <div> tags.

Now that the CSS rules for the major layout areas are defined, let's add them to the page, starting with the #header.

8   Select the placeholder text, Content for id "wrapper" Goes Here, and press Delete (Windows) or forward delete (MacOS) to remove it.

The #wrapper <div> tag typically contains only other <div> tags and no other text or images by themselves.

9   From the Insert bar, click Insert Div Tag. In the Insert Div Tag dialog box, choose After start of tag from the Insert list and then choose <div id="wrapper"> from the adjacent list. From the ID list, choose header and click OK.

By inserting the #header <div> tag after the start of the #wrapper <div> tag, you are nesting one <div> tag inside another and your code will look like this:

```
<div id="wrapper>
        <div id="header"> Content for id "header" Goes Here
        </div>
</div>
```

Now, let's add the next two layout <div> tags, each contained within the #wrapper <div> tag.

10 From the Insert bar, click Insert Div Tag. In the Insert Div Tag dialog box, choose After tag from the Insert list and then choose <div id="header"> from the adjacent list. From the ID list, choose content and click OK.

Notice that each time you choose an item from the ID, only the unassigned ID selectors are available. By limiting your choices, Dreamweaver prevents you from re-using an ID CSS rule.

11 From the Insert bar, click Insert Div Tag. In the Insert Div Tag dialog box, choose After tag from the Insert list and then choose <div id="content"> from the adjacent list. From the ID list, choose footer and click OK.

The placeholder text makes it easy to see where each major layout division is situated.

12 In the Title field of the Document toolbar, enter **Layout** and press Enter (Windows) or Return (MacOS). Choose File > Save.

In the next exercise, you'll begin to expand on the basic layout by including a number of more targeted content areas.

Adding content areas

While it's entirely possible to use the basic layout you've constructed so far in this lesson, the resulting page might be a little bland. More sophisticated designs include additional content areas that are placed adjacent to a layout <div> tag or nested within one; in this exercise, you'll work with both scenarios.

1 If necessary, re-open the layout_start.htm file worked on in the previous exercise by double-clicking its entry in the Files panel.

First, let's define the CSS rule for a <div> tag to hold the logo.

2 In the CSS Styles panel, click New CSS Rule. When the New CSS Rule dialog box is displayed, enter **#logo** in the Selector field. Verify that Selector Type: Advanced and Define in: This document only are chosen and click OK.

In this design, the logo is a background image and so a height must be specified so the full graphic will be seen. A little bit of padding is also needed to separate the logo from other elements.

3 When the CSS Rule Definition for #logo dialog box opens, click Box in the Category column. In the Height field, enter **71** and press Tab. In the Padding area, clear the Same for all checkbox and, in the Bottom field enter **12**. Click OK.

Let's add the <div> tag in its proper place: within the #header <div> tag.

4 From the Insert bar, click Insert Div Tag. In the Insert Div Tag dialog box, choose After start of tag from the Insert list and then choose <div id="header"> from the adjacent list. From the ID list, choose logo and click OK.

Since you've started to put content in the header <div> tag, the placeholder text is no longer needed and can be removed.

5   Select the placeholder text, Content for id "header" Goes Here, and press Delete (Windows) or forward delete (MacOS).

Let's add one more styled element to the #header <div> tag, an area to hold the main navigation. Since the CSS rule is quite similar to that of #logo, you can take the Duplicate shortcut.

6   In the CSS Styles panel, right-click (Windows) or Ctrl+click (MacOS) on the #logo style and choose Duplicate from the pop-up menu. When the Duplicate CSS Rule dialog box is displayed, enter **#nav** in the Selector field and click OK.

Let's specify a different height for the #nav div tag and eliminate the unneeded padding-bottom property.

7   In the CSS Styles panel, select #nav. In the CSS Styles Properties pane, first change the height value from 71 to **28** then select the padding-bottom property and press Delete (Windows) or forward delete (MacOS).

The #nav <div> tag will also be nested within the #header <div> tag, but also—and more importantly—directly after the #logo <div> tag.

8   From the Insert bar, click Insert Div Tag. In the Insert Div Tag dialog box, choose After tag from the Insert list and then choose <div id="logo"> from the adjacent list. From the ID list, choose nav and click OK.

Not all content areas are nested within primary layout <div> tags. Next, you'll create a style for a banner that will be placed between the header and content areas. Again, the quickest way is to duplicate an existing style and modify it.

9   In the CSS Styles panel, right-click (Windows) or Ctrl+click (MacOS) on the #nav style and choose Duplicate from the pop-up menu. When the Duplicate CSS Rule dialog box is displayed, enter **#banner** in the Selector field and click OK.

10 In the CSS Styles panel, select #banner. In the CSS Styles Properties pane, first change the height value from 28 to **200**.

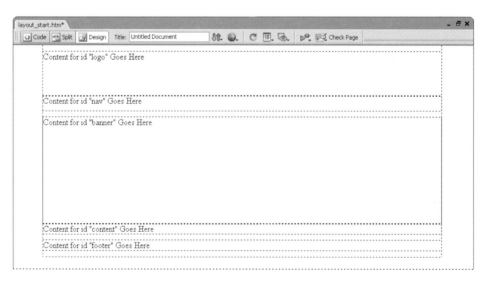

11 From the Insert bar, click Insert Div Tag. In the Insert Div Tag dialog box, choose After tag from the Insert list and then choose <div id="header"> from the adjacent list. From the ID list, choose banner and click OK.

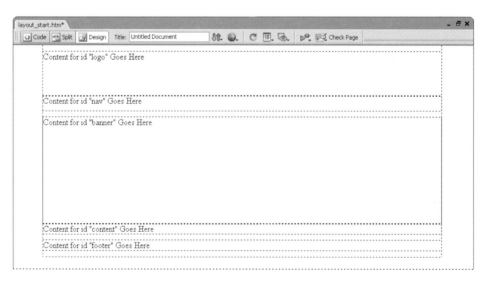

The page is really beginning to take shape now! The next evolution of the design is to separate the content area into two columns. To accomplish this goal, you'll need to first define a style for each column.

12 In the CSS Styles panel, click New CSS Rule. When the New CSS Rule dialog box is displayed, enter **#leftColumn** in the Selector field. Verify that Selector Type: Advanced and Define in: This document only are chosen and click OK.

13 When the CSS Rule Definition for #leftColumn dialog box opens, click Box in the Category column. In the Width field, enter **365** and press Tab. From the Float list, choose left. Click OK.

To create columns with CSS, one key technique is to use the float property. As you may remember, a floated element moves to one side of the containing element and allows other content to flow around it. This is how right-aligned or left-aligned images—and columns—are styled.

By design, these columns are quite similar, so the Duplicate method is again fastest.

14 In the CSS Styles panel, right-click (Windows) or Ctrl+click (MacOS) on the #leftColumn style and choose Duplicate from the pop-up menu. When the Duplicate CSS Rule dialog box is displayed, enter **#rightColumn** in the Selector field and click OK.

15 In the CSS Styles panel, select #rightColumn. In the CSS Styles Properties pane, change the float value from left to right.

You're almost done! The final steps in this portion of the exercise are to create the styled <div> tags.

16 From the Insert bar, click Insert Div Tag. In the Insert Div Tag dialog box, choose After start of tag from the Insert list and then choose <div id="content"> from the adjacent list. From the ID list, choose leftColumn and click OK.

Like the #logo <div> tag, the #rightColumn is within a containing tag, #content, and follows another nested <div> tag, #leftColumn.

17 Click Insert Div Tag again. In the Insert Div Tag dialog box, choose After tag from the Insert list and then choose <div id="leftColumn"> from the adjacent list. From the ID list, choose rightColumn and click OK.

All that's left is a little clean-up.

18 Select the placeholder text, Content for id "content" Goes Here, and press Delete (Windows) or forward delete (MacOS).

19 Choose File > Save.

Although you could hand this page as it stands to a designer, it might take a bit of effort to figure out what you had intended. A good way to create a clean layout design, ready for content, is to add more visual placeholders—a task you'll undertake in the next exercise.

Inserting placeholders

In this exercise, you'll flesh out the layout design with two kinds of placeholder content: image and text.

1 If necessary, re-open the layout_start.htm file worked on in the previous exercise by double-clicking its entry in the Files panel.

2 Select the placeholder text, Content for id "logo" Goes Here, and press Delete (Windows) or forward delete (MacOS). In the Common category of the Insert bar, select Image Placeholder () from the Images menu button.

3 When the Image Placeholder dialog box opens, enter **Logo** in the Name field, **760** in the Width field and **71** in the Height field. Leave all the other fields at their default values and click OK.

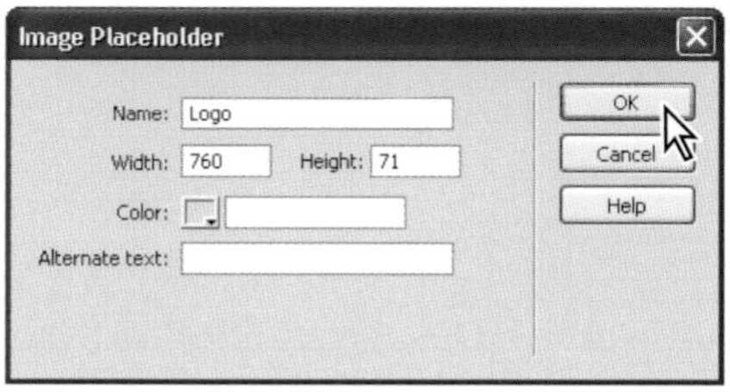

The same process is used to create placeholders for the #nav and #banner <div> tags.

4 Repeat steps 2 and 3 to replace the placeholder text in the #nav <div> tag with an image placeholder with the name **Navigation**, a width of **760** and height of **28**.

5   Repeat steps 2 and 3 one last time to replace the placeholder text in the #banner
<div> tag with an image placeholder with the name Banner, a width of **760** and height
of **200**.

With the graphic placeholders inserted, let's add some basic placeholder text, starting
with a headline that spans both columns.

6   Place your cursor in the placeholder text Content for id "leftColumn" Goes Here
and, from the Tag Selector, choose <div #leftColumn>. Press left-arrow to move your
cursor between #content <div> tag and the #leftColumn <div> tag and enter **Main
Heading**. Choose Window > Properties to open the Property inspector and, from the
Format list, choose Heading 1.

7 Select the placeholder text Content for id "leftColumn" Goes Here and press Delete (Windows) or forward delete (MacOS). Enter **Subheading**. In the Property inspector, choose Heading 2 from the Format list. Place your cursor after the just entered text and press Enter (Windows) or Return (MacOS) to create a new line below the heading.

To spare you the chore of typing in a paragraph of placeholder text, I've included a file that you can copy and paste onto the page.

8 Place your cursor after the word **Subheading** and press Enter (Windows) or Return (MacOS). From the Files panel, expand lesson07 and double-click placeholder_text. htm to open it. Choose Edit > Select All and then press Ctrl+C (Windows) or Cmd+C (MacOS); when you're done, choose File > Close. When you return to layout_start.htm, press Ctrl+V (Windows) or Cmd+V (MacOS) to paste the copied text.

Let's put the exact same content in the right column with a quick and easy shortcut.

9 With your cursor in the left column, choose Edit > Select All. Notice that only the text within the #leftColumn <div> tag is selected. Press Ctrl+C (Windows) or Cmd+C (MacOS). Select the placeholder text Content for id "rightColumn" Goes Here and press Ctrl+V (Windows) or Cmd+V (MacOS) to paste the copied content.

In Dreamweaver, the Select All command initially selects the content within a container, such as text in a table cell or content in a <div> tag. This allows you to quickly copy or move content from one location to another. Repeat the command once more to select the container and a third time to select everything on the page.

10 Choose File > Save.

Now your layout design is both structurally sound and easy to follow. Congratulations!

Exporting CSS styles

The layout page worked on in the previous exercises is now complete unto itself. However, before this page is put into production, it's a good idea to move the CSS styles from the <head> of the document to an external CSS style sheet. Dreamweaver offers a command to handle that task quickly and easily.

1 If necessary, re-open the layout_start.htm file worked on in the previous exercise by double-clicking its entry in the Files panel.

2 In the CSS Styles panel, select the first defined style, body, press Shift and select the last style, #rightColumn.

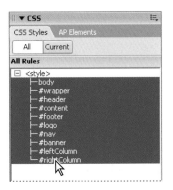

3 From the CSS Styles panel Options menu, choose Move Rules.

You can also right-click (Windows) or Ctrl+click (MacOS) to reach the same menu option.

4   When the Move to External Style Sheet dialog box opens, select the Move Rules To A new style sheet option and click OK.

5   In the Save Style Sheet File As dialog box, navigate to the lesson07 > css folder and, in the File Name field, enter **main.css**. Click Save when you're done.

Dreamweaver moves the selected styles from the <head> area to the newly defined style sheet and, simultaneously, inserts a link to the style sheet from the current document. The last chore—admittedly optional—is to remove the no longer needed <style> tag.

6   In the CSS Styles panel, click the <style> entry and press Delete (Windows) or forward delete (MacOS).

7   Choose File > Save All.

In the next exercise, you'll learn how to use Dreamweaver's ruler and guides to make adjustments to your layouts, as needed.

Using the Ruler and Guides

Designs are rarely static. Changes can come from any quarter—the client, an art director, even your own creative impulses. Dreamweaver provides a range of layout tools intended to help you adapt your designs quickly and easily. In this exercise, you'll use the ruler and guides to visually re-align the content columns with a portion of a graphic.

1 If necessary, re-open the layout_start.htm file worked on in the previous exercise by double-clicking its entry in the Files panel.

2 Press F4 to close any open panels and maximize your workspace.

3 Double-click the Banner image placeholder. When the Select Image Source dialog box opens, navigate to the lesson07 > images folder and select bench.jpg. Click OK.

As with most graphic programs like Photoshop or Fireworks, you'll need to display the rulers before you can use the guides.

4 Choose View > Rulers > Show and then choose View > Rulers > Reset Origin.

💡 *You can change the origin of the ruler by dragging the upper left corner to a new location on the page. Double-click this corner to reset the origin to the upper left corner of the Document window.*

Guides are dragged from the horizontal or vertical rulers as needed.

5   From the vertical ruler on the left edge of the Document window, drag out a guide and align it with the right edge of the bench, approximately 628 pixels from the left.

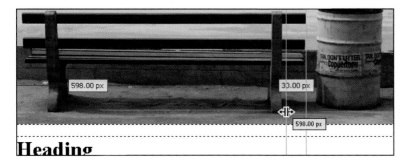

A tooltip displays the pixel distance from the ruler origin on the vertical (or Y) axis. You can adjust the position of the guide by placing your pointer over the guide and, when the two headed arrow appears, drag it to a new location.

Note: This exercise only uses vertical guides; horizontal guides are dragged onto the page from the horizontal ruler along the top of the Document window.

6   Press Ctrl (Windows) or Cmd (MacOS) and drag another vertical guide from the ruler. Note the tooltips with the various pixel dimensions; drag the guide until the two guides are 30 pixels apart.

The dimensions displayed are from one guide to another and from the edge of the Document window. To get the exact measurements you'll need additional guides placed on both the left and right edge of the layout.

💡 *To remove a single guide, drag it off the page in either direction.*

7 Drag a vertical guide to the right edge of the layout; note that the guide snaps into place. Drag a final vertical guide to the left edge of the layout.

With all your guides in place, you're ready to gather the needed dimensions.

8 Place your cursor between the left-most guide and the next guide and press Ctrl (Windows) or Cmd (MacOS): note the displayed dimension, which should be 489 pixels. Move your cursor between the right-most guide and the next guide to the left (on the right edge of the bench); here, the dimension displayed should be 241 pixels.

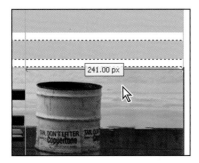

Now, let's adjust the appropriate CSS properties.

9   Choose Window > CSS Styles. In All mode, select #rightColumn and, in the CSS Styles Properties pane, double-click the current value, 365px, and enter **241** and press Enter (Windows) or Return (MacOS). Next, select #leftColumn and in the CSS Styles Properties pane, double-click the current value, 365px, and enter **489** and press Enter (Windows) or Return (MacOS).

Adjustments to the width of two columns maintains the 30 pixel column between them while aligning them with a visual element on the page.

10   Choose View > Guides > Clear Guides and then choose File > Save All. Finally, choose Hide All Visual Aids from the Visual Aids menu button on the Document toolbar and press F4.

Congratulations, you've completed this lesson!

Review

▶ **Review questions**

1   What CSS selector should you use to define zero margins and zero padding? If you want to center your layout, what property and value do you need to include in the CSS rule for backwards compatibility with older browsers?

2   Name two benefits for using a #wrapper <div> tag in a CSS-based layout.

3   Describe the process for inserting a layout styled <div> tag.

4   True or False: The only way to move CSS styles from the <head> of a document to an external style sheet is to cut and paste them.

5   What's the first step to dragging a guide onto the screen?

▶ **Review answers**

1   Use the <body> tag as your selector and, in addition to setting margin: 0 and padding: 0, you should also set text-align: center for a centered layout.

2   A #wrapper <div> tag allows you to set the overall width for the layout in one location and to easily align the layout left, right or center.

3   First, define the CSS layout style, typically with an ID selector, like #header. The style can include any necessary attributes, such as margins, padding, or height. Once the style is created, choose Insert Div Tag from the Common category of the Insert bar; within the Insert Div Tag dialog box, choose where to place the <div> tag—such as after a certain other <div> tag begins—and then select the just-defined ID selector to use.

4   False. Dreamweaver provides the Move CSS Styles command from the Options menu of the CSS Styles panel which can move styles from the <head> of a document to an existing style sheet or a new one.

5   The first step to dragging a guide onto the screen is to display the rulers, by choosing View > Rulers > Show.

dev/design

Home Spirit *Folks* Work Contact

Down time for our hard-working crew

Scenes from our 3rd annual off-site gathering

Lorem ipsum dolor sit amet, consetetur sadipscing elitr, sed diam nonumy eirmod tempor invidunt ut labore et dolore magna aliquyam erat, sed diam voluptua. At vero eos et accusam et justo duo dolores et ea rebum. Stet clita kasd gubergren, no sea takimata sanctus est Lorem ipsum dolor sit amet.

Lorem ipsum dolor sit amet, consetetur sadipscing elitr, sed diam nonumy eirmod tempor invidunt ut labore et dolore magna aliquyam erat, sed diam voluptua. At vero eos et accusam et justo duo dolores et ea rebum. Stet clita kasd gubergren, no sea takimata sanctus est Lorem ipsum dolor sit amet.

?   +

?   +

?   +

What brings a Web page to life? Interactivity. Rollover an image to see another larger image appear instantly, click a link to open a new browser window with additional information or load a page to watch a freshly added section glow momentarily to attract your attention. All of these examples of interactivity are easily accomplished with Dreamweaver behaviors—and, better still, quickly tailored to custom-fit your new, lively Web page.

8 | Creating Interactive Pages

In this lesson, you'll learn how to make your Web pages interactive by doing the following:

- Learn about Dreamweaver Behaviors.
- Apply a behavior to swap an image source.
- Modify an existing behavior.
- Open a browser window, interactively.
- Define areas to show and hide under user control.
- Change the triggering event for a behavior.

This lesson will take about 90 minutes to complete. Be sure you have copied Lessons/Lesson08 from the Adobe Dreamweaver CS3 Classroom in a Book CD to your hard drive before beginning. As you work on this lesson, you'll overwrite the start files. If you need to restore the start files, copy them again from the CD.

Learning about Dreamweaver Behaviors

A Dreamweaver behavior is JavaScript code that performs an action, like opening a browser window, when triggered by a particular event, like, a mouse click. Applying a behavior is a three-step process:

1 Select the page element you want to trigger the behavior.

2 Choose the behavior to apply.

3 Specify the settings or parameters of the behavior.

Typically the triggering element is a linked one, either a range of text or an image. A dummy link is used so another page does not load: dummy links can either be a hash mark (#) or a JavaScript function call without a function, javascript:;. Many developers prefer the latter to avoid issues with older browsers such as Netscape Navigator 4.

Dreamweaver includes over 30 behaviors, all inserted from the Behaviors panel. Some of the functionality available to you through Dreamweaver behaviors includes:

- Calling a custom defined JavaScript function.

- Opening a browser window.

- Swapping an image's source—and swapping it back for a rollover effect.

- Fading an image or page area in and out.

- Growing or shrinking a graphic.

- Popping up a message.

- Changing the text or other HTML within a given area.

- Showing or hiding sections of the page.

Not all behaviors are available all the time. For example, you'll need an image on the page before the Swap Image behavior is enabled on the Behaviors list.

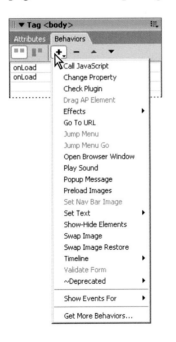

All behaviors display a unique dialog box used to define the relevant settings. For example, the Open Browser Window dialog box allows you to set the Web address of the file to display in the new window, the width and height of the window as well as other window attributes. The chosen parameters can be modified at any time.

Once you've defined the parameters of your behavior, it is listed in the Behaviors panel with the default triggering action on the left and the name of the behavior on the right. The action can be altered by choosing a different one from the list. For example, the Show-Hide Elements behavior, by default, applies an onClick action; if you'd prefer a rollover trigger, you can change the action to onMouseOver.

Behaviors are extremely flexible. Multiple behaviors can be applied to the same trigger; you could, for example, swap one image for another and then change the text of the accompanying image caption, all with one click. Although it happens so fast, it may seem like the events are simultaneous, behaviors are actually triggered in sequence. When multiple behaviors with the same triggering event are applied, you'll have the option to change the order in which the behaviors occur by moving them up or down in the Behaviors panel.

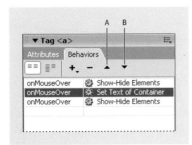

A. *Move behavior up*
B. *Move behavior down*

Previewing your completed file

To get a sense of the file you will work on in the first part of this lesson, let's preview the completed page in the browser.

1   Start Adobe Dreamweaver CS3.

2   If necessary, press F8 to open the Files panel and choose DW CIB from the site list.

3   In the Files panel, expand the lesson08 folder.

4   Select the behaviors_final.htm file and press F12 (Windows) or Option+F12 (MacOS) to preview it in your primary browser.

The page includes a number of interactive effects, all created with Dreamweaver behaviors.

5   If Internet Explorer is your primary browser and a message appears on top of the browser window that indicates that JavaScript are being prevented from running, click the message bar and choose Allow Blocked Content.

6   Move your cursor over each of the small images on the right; note that the large image changes to give you an enhanced view.

7   Move your cursor over the question mark under the first small image to see an in-picture caption appear. Move your cursor away to hide the caption. Repeat these actions with the other images to see their captions.

8   Click the plus sign under the first small picture; note the new browser window that appears with the enlarged image. Close the new browser window. Click the plus signs under the other images to view their larger views.

9   When you're done, close all browser windows and return to Dreamweaver.

Applying behaviors

One of the most common effects on the Web is the rollover. In a rollover, when the site visitor's cursor moves over a particular graphic, a different graphic appears, typically with just a few aspects changed to give the effect of the image rolling over to another state. Under the hood, a rollover is basically a behavior that exchanges one image source for another. However, Dreamweaver's Swap Image behavior can handle much more than simple rollovers. In this exercise, you'll add a Swap Image behavior to the page that temporarily replaces the main image on the page with a larger version of the thumbnail image when the visitor's cursor moves over the thumbnail.

1   From the Files panel, expand the lesson08 folder and double-click the behaviors_ start.htm file to open it.

The Swap Image behavior requires that the targeted image be identified with a unique name. Let's add that name now.

2   Select the figure on the left of the page. In the Property inspector, enter
mediumImage in the Name field, located between the small thumbnail and the image
dimensions.

Next, let's prepare the page element to act as the behavior's trigger.

3   Select the middle image in the right column.

4   If necessary, choose Window > Properties to display the Property inspector.

For the widest cross-browser compatibility, you need to apply your behavior to a link
surrounding an image or text phrase. However, because you don't want to link to
another page, a dummy link is used instead.

5 In the Link field of the Property inspector, enter **javascript:;** and press Tab.

As mentioned earlier, javascript:; is a JavaScript function call without a function; be sure to type the trailing colon and semicolon after the word javascript.

There's one more task before you can apply the behavior: you need to select the triggering element.

6 From the Tag Selector, select the <a> tag.

7 Choose Window > Behaviors to open the Behaviors panel.

8 Click Add (⊞), the plus sign, and, from the list, select Swap Image.

9   When the Swap Image dialog box appears, scroll down to the bottom of the Images list and select image "mediumImage".

10   Click Browse. When the Select Image Source dialog box opens, navigate to the lesson08 > images folder and select splash_medium.jpg; click OK (Windows) or Choose (MacOS). Make sure that both the Preload images and Restore images onMouseOut options are selected and click OK to close the Swap Image dialog box.

Two behaviors appear in the Behaviors panel: Swap Image and Swap Image Restore. Dreamweaver applies both behaviors in order to achieve the full rollover effect.

Now let's repeat the procedure for the bottom image.

Note: There's no need to apply the Swap Image behavior to the top image in the right column because it is also the default large image and already on view.

11   Select the bottom image in the right column. In the Property inspector, enter **javascript:;** in the Link field and press Tab.

12   From the Tag Selector, choose <a>

13   In the Behaviors panel, click Add and, from the list, select Swap Image.

14   When the Swap Image dialog box appears, scroll down to the bottom of the Images list and select image "mediumImage".

Because you're swapping the source of the same image, you choose the same image name as before.

15 Click Browse. When the Select Image Source dialog box opens, navigate to the lesson08 > images folder and select dog_medium.jpg; click OK (Windows) or Choose (MacOS). Make sure that both the Preload images and Restore images onMouseOut options are selected and click OK to close the Swap Image dialog box.

16 Choose File > Save and press F12 (Windows) or Option+F12 (MacOS) to preview the page in your primary browser. Move your cursor over the thumbnail images to view the changes in the central image. When you're done, close your browser and return to Dreamweaver.

Now you have two separate targets—two thumbnails in the right column—that interactively change the image source of a single image. Without increasing the amount of space used on the page, you're now able to display multiple images, on demand.

Opening browser windows

Pop-up windows—smaller browser windows that open from a main browser page—are a common effect on the Web. Dreamweaver's Open Browser Window behavior adds this functionality to any Web page, with a high degree of control over the browser window controls.

1 If necessary, re-open the behaviors_start.htm file worked on in the previous exercise by double-clicking its entry in the Files panel.

The plus sign beneath each image will be used to launch the new window.

2 Select the plus sign underneath the first thumbnail image in the right column.

3 In the Property inspector, enter **javascript:;** in the Link field and press Tab.

4 From the Behaviors panel, click Add and choose Open Browser Window from the list.

5 When the Open Browser Window dialog box appears, click Browse. From the Select Image Source dialog box, navigate to the lesson08 > images folder and select group_large.jpg; click OK (Windows) or Choose (MacOS).

The Open Browser Window dialog box is often used to display entire HTML pages, in this circumstance, however, a single image is shown.

6 In the Open Browser Window dialog box, enter **820** in the Window width field and **550** in the Window height field. Check the Location toolbar checkbox and click OK.

The actual image dimensions are 800 x 530, but slightly larger width and height are applied to account for the browser window chrome. Dreamweaver offers a wide range of browser control options; here, the location toolbar is selected to allow viewers to copy the link and forward to friends.

Note: The Window name field is used for advanced JavaScript functions and its use is optional.

7   Choose File > Save and press F12 (Windows) or Option+F12 (MacOS) to preview the page in your primary browser.

8   If Internet Explorer is your primary browser and a message appears on top of the browser window that indicates that scripts are prevented from running, click the message bar and choose Allow Blocked Content.

9   Click on the plus sign beneath the first image. After you've viewed the larger image in the new window, close it and your browser to return to Dreamweaver.

Rather than repeat the same steps for the other two thumbnails, in the next exercise you'll learn a shortcut that takes advantage of Dreamweaver's ability to modify existing behaviors.

Modifying a behavior

Getting the desired effect from a behavior often requires a good bit of trial and error. You might, for example, need to find just the right width and height for a pop-up browser window. Luckily, you can easily re-open the dialog box of any behavior and make any necessary changes—an ability which you will put to your advantage in this exercise.

1   If necessary, re-open the behaviors_start.htm file worked on in the previous exercise by double-clicking its entry in the Files panel.

2   Select the plus sign under the first thumbnail image in the column on the right. Press Ctrl+C (Windows) or Cmd+C (MacOS) to copy the selection.

The goal in this exercise is to quickly replicate the behavior inserted in the previous exercise by first copying and pasting the needed code and then modifying the behavior as needed.

3 Select the plus sign under the second thumbnail image and press Ctrl+V (Windows) or Cmd+V (MacOS).

4 If the Behaviors panel is not available, choose Window > Behaviors to show it.

5 Double-click the behavior name, Open Browser Window, in the right column of the Behaviors panel to re-open the dialog box.

6 In the Open Browser Window dialog box, click Browse and navigate to the lesson08 > images folder and select splash_large.jpg; click OK (Windows) or Choose (MacOS). Leave all the other options at their current settings and click OK.

Open Browser Window

URL to display: images/group_large.jpg   [Browse...]   [OK]   [Cancel]   [Help]

Window width: 820   Window height: 550

Attributes: ☐ Navigation toolbar   ☐ Menu bar
             ☑ Location toolbar   ☐ Scrollbars as needed
             ☐ Status bar   ☐ Resize handles

Window name:

The same text link (the plus sign) is used for all behavior event triggers and the only variation is the file name that is being interactively shown. Let's finish up this behavior by repeating the previous steps to add the behavior to the final image.

7 Select the plus sign under the third thumbnail image and press Ctrl+V (Windows) or Cmd+V (MacOS).

8　Double-click the behavior name, Open Browser Window, in the right column of the Behaviors panel to re-open the dialog box.

9　In the Open Browser Window dialog box, click Browse and navigate to the lesson08 > images folder and select dog_large.jpg; click OK (Windows) or Choose (MacOS). Leave all the other options at their current settings and click OK.

10　Choose File > Save and then press F12 (Windows) or Option+F12 (MacOS) to preview the page in your primary browser. Click the plus signs under any of the images to see an enlarged version of that graphic.

11　When you're done, close all your browser windows and return to Dreamweaver.

The page is really shaping up, interactively. With two different sets of behaviors applied to various targets, the page visitor can now quickly view a medium size image by rolling over the thumbnails and, with a click, examine a large size image. In the next exercise, you'll apply another behavior that allows you to show and hide page elements.

Showing and hiding areas

One trend in Web design is to only display some information on an as-needed basis. Typically, this entails revealing a previously hidden page element, such as a <div> tag with some relevant content; when the information is no longer needed, the page element is again hidden. In this exercise, you'll apply Dreamweaver's Show-Hide Elements behavior to interactively display captions for each of the thumbnail images.

1   If necessary, re-open the behaviors_start.htm file worked on in the previous exercise by double-clicking its entry in the Files panel.

This page already includes the necessary images with captions, each placed in an absolutely positioned <div> tag, referred to in Dreamweaver as an AP element. The caption images are hidden by default.

2   Select the question mark underneath the first thumbnail in the right column. Make sure to include the two non-breaking spaces placed after the question mark in your selection.

If you're unsure if you've selected correctly, switch to Split view to verify that you've selected the following code: ? .

Because this behavior will be triggered by onMouseOver and onMouseOut events, a slightly larger target area than the single character makes it easier to use.

3   If the Property inspector is not displayed, choose Window > Properties. In the Link field, enter **javascript:;** and press Tab.

4   From the Behaviors panel, choose Add and select Show-Hide Elements from the list.

5 When the Show-Hide Elements dialog box appears, scroll down the Elements list until you locate div "appDiv1". Select it and click Show; when you're done, click OK.

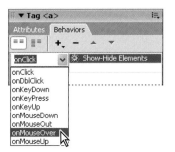

By default, the Show-Hide Elements behavior inserts an onClick event. This scenario requires a rollover type of interactivity, so you'll need to change the event to one that is more suitable.

6 In the Behaviors panel, click onClick next to the just added behavior and, from the list, select onMouseOver.

Unlike the Swap Image behavior, the Show-Hide Elements behavior does not include an option to restore the element to its previous state. The solution is to apply the behavior again, with a different action and event.

7 From the Behaviors panel, choose Add and select Show-Hide Elements from the list.

8   When the Show-Hide Elements dialog box appears, scroll down the Elements list until you locate div "appDiv1". Select it and click Hide; when you're done, click OK.

Just as you change the show element event to onMouseOver, now you change the hide element event to onMouseOut.

9   In the Behaviors panel, click onClick next to the just added behavior and, from the list, select onMouseOut.

While you can use the same copy and paste technique to add the behaviors to the other question marks, it's actually a bit faster to apply them from the ground up.

10   Select the question mark underneath the second thumbnail in the right column. Again, make sure to include the two non-breaking spaces placed after the question mark in your selection.

11   From the Property inspector, enter **javascript:;** in the Link field and press Tab.

12 From the Behaviors panel, choose Add and select Show-Hide Elements from the list.

13 When the Show-Hide Elements dialog box appears, scroll down the Elements list until you locate div "appDiv2". Select it and click Show; when you're done, click OK.

14 In the Behaviors panel, click onClick next to the just added behavior and, from the list, select onMouseOver.

Now let's add the behavior to hide the caption when the visitor's cursor moves away from the targeted link.

15 From the Behaviors panel, choose Add and select Show-Hide Elements from the list.

16 When the Show-Hide Elements dialog box appears, scroll down the Elements list until you locate div "appDiv2". Select it and click Hide; when you're done, click OK.

Just as you change the show element event to onMouseOver, now you change the hide element event to onMouseOut.

17 In the Behaviors panel, click onClick next to the just added behavior and, from the list, select onMouseOut.

Two down, one to go! Let's add the same behaviors for the third and final thumbnail image.

18 Select the question mark underneath the third thumbnail in the right column. Once again, make sure to include the two non-breaking spaces placed after the question mark in your selection.

19 From the Property inspector, enter **javascript:;** in the Link field and press Tab.

20 From the Behaviors panel, choose Add and select Show-Hide Elements from the list.

21 When the Show-Hide Elements dialog box appears, scroll down the Elements list until you locate div "appDiv3". Select it and click Show; when you're done, click OK.

22 In the Behaviors panel, click onClick next to the just added behavior and, from the list, select onMouseOver.

Now let's add the behavior to hide the caption when the visitor's cursor moves away from the targeted link.

23 From the Behaviors panel, choose Add and select Show-Hide Elements from the list.

24 When the Show-Hide Elements dialog box appears, scroll down the Elements list until you locate div "appDiv3". Select it and click Hide; when you're done, click OK.

Last update to the page: modify the hide element event to onMouseOut.

25 In the Behaviors panel, click onClick next to the just added behavior and, from the list, select onMouseOut.

26 Choose File > Save and press F12 (Windows) or Option+F12 (MacOS) to preview the page in your primary browser. Move your cursor over the question mark under the first thumbnail to reveal the caption; move your cursor away to hide it. Repeat with the other question marks to view the associated captions. When you're done, close your browser and return to Dreamweaver.

Congratulations, you've completed this lesson!

Review

▶ **Review questions**

1 Name the two component parts of a Dreamweaver behavior and describe them.

2 Are all behaviors always available?

3 What do I need to apply a behavior?

4 Can behaviors be modified once installed? If so, how?

5 What is a quick way to apply the same behavior to the same text phrase but with different settings?

▶ **Review answers**

1 A Dreamweaver behavior is composed of an event and an action. An event is what triggers the behavior; examples of events are onClick, onMouseOver, and onLoad. An action is what happens in a behavior. Example actions are opening a browser window, swapping an image source or showing/hiding elements.

2 No. Certain behaviors require certain page elements to exist on the page to be enabled on the Behaviors panel list. For example, you'd need a linked image on the page before the Swap Image Source dialog box is enabled.

3 A trigger of some sort, typically a linked image or text phrase with a dummy link, like javascript:; or a hash mark, #.

4 Yes, you can easily modify your behavior settings by double-clicking on the behavior name in the Behaviors panel to re-open the associated dialog box.

5 Apply the behavior to the first page element and then copy the page element. Paste the page element in the appropriate place and, from the Behaviors panel, double-click the behavior to open the dialog box for parameter customization.

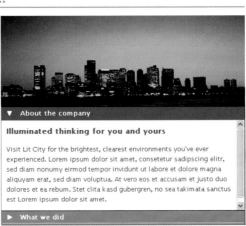

Welcome to the world of Web 2.0. Here, portions of pages are updated with XML data—without reloading the entire page. Here, content on a page is hidden or revealed at the click of a mouse button. Here, sophisticated effects highlight a designated area automatically when the page is loaded—and disappear without further interaction. Dreamweaver CS3 brings you Web 2.0 power with a full range of easy-to-use tools to control the Adobe Ajax framework, Spry.

9 | Integrating Ajax with Spry

In this lesson, you'll learn how to add Web 2.0 functionality to your Web pages interactive by doing the following:

- Learn about Ajax and Spry from Adobe.
- Work with XML data.
- Attach an XML data source to your page.
- Insert a Spry table.
- Include a Spry Accordion widget.
- Apply a Spry effect.

This lesson will take about 90 minutes to complete. Be sure you have copied Lessons/Lesson09 from the Adobe Dreamweaver CS3 Classroom in a Book CD to your hard drive before beginning. As you work on this lesson, you'll overwrite the start files. If you need to restore the start files, copy them again from the CD.

Learning about Ajax and Spry

Leading Web designers have recently touted the arrival of Web 2.0, a new era in Internet usability and interactivity. The prime technology driving Web 2.0 is known as Ajax-- Asynchronous JavaScript and XML. If you've ever scrolled through a Google Map or browsed a photo collection on Flickr, you've experienced what Ajax can do.

The key term in the Ajax acronym is asynchronous, which literally means "not at the same time." Normally, the viewing of pages on the Web is a very linear process. For example, let's say you're reviewing information on a site about a particular company. Here's what happens in a standard Web site:

1   You visit a page with your browser.

2   The initial page is sent from a remote Web server.

3   Your browser renders the page.

4   You click a link on the page to learn more.

5   Your browser requests a new page with additional information from the remote Web server.

6   The Web server sends the new page.

7   Your browser loads the page that includes the new details and displays an entirely new page.

Here's how the same operation would work with an Ajax-driven page:

1   You visit a page with your browser.

2   The initial page is sent from a remote Web server.

3   Your browser renders the page and, simultaneously, loads all related data into the Ajax engine.

4   You click a link on the page to learn more.

5   Acting like a middleman, the Ajax engine catches the new request and returns any relevant details.

6   Your browser displays the new details on the existing page and updates only the relevant section of the page.

Essentially, Ajax loads relevant data for a page but does not display it until requested. This makes the user experience much smoother and more interactive. Should more data be required than was initially loaded, the Ajax engine downloads the data from the Web server in the background and then delivers it to the browser for display as needed.

Most implementations of Ajax require an advanced knowledge of JavaScript and a great deal of hand-coding. To ease the learning curve, Adobe has developed an Ajax framework known as Spry that integrates seamlessly with Dreamweaver CS3. There are four different sets of Spry tools:

• Spry Data – Incorporates XML data into any Web page and allows for the Ajax-style interactive display of data.

• Spry Form widgets – Combines form elements, like text fields and lists, with JavaScript validation functions and user-friendly error messages.

• Spry Layout widgets – Provides a series of sophisticated layout controls, including tabbed and accordion panels.

• Spry Effects – Extends the Dreamweaver behavior library with advanced functionality to interactively affect page elements; Spry effects include the ability to fade, reveal, slide, highlight and shake targeted page components.

 In this lesson, you'll have an opportunity to experience the power of Spry firsthand.

Note: If you'd like to peek under the hood and learn more about how Spry works, visit Adobe Labs (http://labs.adobe.com/technologies/spry/).

Previewing your completed file

To get a sense of the file you will work on in the first part of this lesson, let's preview the completed page in the browser.

1 Start Adobe Dreamweaver CS3.

2 If necessary, press F8 to open the Files panel and choose DW CIB from the site list.

3 In the Files panel, expand the lesson09 folder.

4   Select the spry_final.htm file and press F12 (Windows) or Option+F12 (MacOS) to preview it in your primary browser.

The page includes a variety of Ajax-powered effects, all created with Dreamweaver Spry technology.

Note: If Internet Explorer 7 is your primary browser, you'll need to take some additional steps to view the Spry dynamic content locally. First, your site must be within the local server Web root; be sure your Lessons folder is stored in the Inetpub > wwwroot folder. Next, double-click the site name in the Files panel to open the Site Definition dialog. Click the Testing Server category; from the Access list, choose Local/Network. Click OK to close the Site Definition dialog. Now, when you preview your page with Internet Explorer, your local Web server (localhost) serves the page as designed.

When the page initially loads, you'll notice a yellow background color highlights the primary headline for a brief period and then disappears; this is the result of a Spry effect called Highlight.

5   Click the column header Since once to sort the data by the year in an ascending order; click it again to sort the data by year in a descending order. Click the column header Company to present the data in alphabetical order.

6   Move your cursor over the various entries in the table of data in the left column. Click the last entry in the table.

When you select any data entry from the data table, the associated image appears in the right column and related details are displayed in the accordion panel below the figure.

7 Click the bottom accordion panel tab, What we did. Note the new information reveal. Click the top accordion panel tab, About the company, to see the information in that content area.

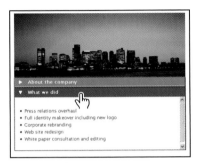

8 Continue exploring by clicking the data entries in the left column and the accordion panel tabs in the right.

9 When you're done, close all browser windows and return to Dreamweaver.

Including XML data

Before you can display any data with Spry, you'll need to establish a proper XML data source. XML, short for Extensible Markup Language, is a standardized format for maintaining data, often in a text file. Each XML file can contain multiple data records. For example, in this exercise you'll work with an XML file that holds data for a number of clients. Each client record, without the data, looks like this:

```
<client>
      <company></company>
      <desc></desc>
      <pic></pic>
      <work></work>
      <startdate></startdate>
</client>
```

As you'll see in this exercise, this XML structure is referred to as the schema. The actual data is placed between the opening and closing tag pairs, like this:

```
<company>Company Anon</company>
```

Data which has the potential for using special characters, such as the angle brackets used to surround tags, rely on a special delimiter for character data that is used like this:

```
<desc>![CDATA[Company Anon is a <strong>bold</strong>
company.]]</desc>
```

The CDATA delimiter allows XML data to contain HTML tags. For example, this XML file used in this exercise includes a fully formatted HTML unordered list.

Dreamweaver's direct route for working with the XML schema is the Spry Data object, which you will work with in the following steps.

1   From the Files panel, expand the lesson09 folder and double-click the spry_start. htm file to open it.

2   In the Insert bar, switch to the Spry category either by choosing Spry from the Insert bar list or clicking the Spry tab.

3   From the Spry category, click Spry Data (🗋), the first icon on the left of the toolbar.

4 When the Spry XML Data Set dialog box opens, leave the default Data Set name, ds1, and click Browse. In the Select XML Source dialog box, navigate to the lesson09 folder and choose clients.xml; click OK (Windows) or Choose (MacOS) to close the just-opened dialog box.

5 With the Spry XML Data Set dialog still open, click Get schema. When the schema is displayed in the Row element area, click the repeating entry, client.

💡 *Repeating entries are designated with a plus sign next to the HTML angle brackets (◈).*

6 Click Preview to verify your data is available. When the Data preview Spry XML Data Set dialog box opens, review your data; click OK when you're done.

Next, you'll change the data types for a couple of the data columns.

7   In the Data Set columns area, select the pic data column and, from the Data type list, choose image link. Select the startdate data column and, from the Data type list, choose number.

XPath:	clients/client		Preview...

Data Set columns:	Column	Data Type
	desc	string
	pic	image link
	work	string
	startdate	number

Data type: number

Sort: company   Direction: Ascending

Options: ☐ Distinct on load
☐ Turn XML Data Caching Off
☐ Auto refresh data [   ] milliseconds

Spry Data Types

The proper data type is necessary for sorting operations. In the next exercise, you'll insert a Spry table that includes the option for sortable table columns; if the data columns are not set to the correct data type, the columns will not sort correctly. For example, if a data column with number values remains with the default string data type, the numbers could potentially not be ordered sequentially.

The available data types are:

- string – Any alphanumeric data.
- number – Any numeric data.
- date – Any full date, such as 6/13/2007 or June 13, 2007.
- image link – Any file name or path intended to be used as an image src value.

8   From the Sort list, choose company. Leave the remaining options at their default setting and click OK.

Dreamweaver needs to include a couple of JavaScript files for Spry data functionality to work properly and displays an alert to remind you that these files—stored in the SpryAssets folder—must be uploaded for the page to work properly.

9 Choose File > Save.

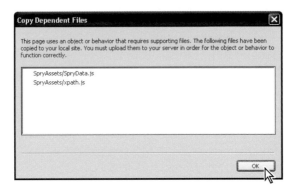

10 When the Copy Dependent Files dialog box appears, review the files you'll need to upload and click OK.

Although there is no obvious change in Design view, Dreamweaver has inserted a number of key code lines. In addition to the previously noted JavaScript files, a JavaScript function is included in the <head> tag:

```
var ds1 = new Spry.Data.XMLDataSet("clients.xml", "clients/clien
t",{sortOnLoad:"company",sortOrderOnLoad:"ascending"});

ds1.setColumnType("pic", "image");

ds1.setColumnType("startdate", "number");
```

This JavaScript function applies all the parameters chosen in the Spry XML Data Set dialog box, including the column types.

In the next exercise, you'll put the Spry data connection to use by inserting a Spry table object.

Building Spry data sets

The data from a Spry XML data connection on the page is often presented in a simple two-row table. The top row of the table contains the column headers, which can optionally sort the data below. The second row of the table holds the data variables that, when the page is browsed, are replaced by the actual data values. The second table row tag includes an attribute which causes the row to repeat as many times as necessary to display all the data. Other attributes to style the odd and even rows differently or to change styles when the page visitor's mouse hovers over a row or selects it are also optionally placed in the second <tr> tag.

Coding such a data-connected table by hand is entirely possible, but quite tedious and requires in-depth understanding of Spry attributes and values. Luckily, Dreamweaver includes an object—the Spry Table—which creates the entire table in one operation, without touching the code. The Spry Table displays a master list of the available data with just enough information to identify the data record. Another area on the page—the detail region—is necessary to show additional related data, including associated images and text.

Adding a Spry Table

In this exercise, you'll insert a Spry Table onto the page, configured to show your XML data when previewed in a master region.

1   If necessary, re-open the spry_start.htm file worked on in the previous exercise by double-clicking its entry in the Files panel.

2   Select the placeholder text Data placeholder and press Delete (Windows) or forward delete (MacOS).

3   From the Spry category of the Insert bar, click Spry Table (🖳), the fifth icon from the left.

The first major task in the Insert Spry Table dialog box is to choose which data columns to display. As all available columns are shown initially, this task is a process of elimination where you remove those columns you do not wish to show.

4   When the Insert Spry Table dialog box opens, make sure the Spry Data Set selection is ds1. In the Columns area, choose tagline and click Remove (▭). Continue clicking Remove to delete the desc, pic, and work data columns.

When you're finished removing data columns, there should be just two remaining: company and startdate. Now, let's make both of those columns sortable.

5   Select company and check the Sort column when header is clicked checkbox. Repeat the operation with startdate selected.

Next, you'll assign a series of CSS classes to style the data.

6   From the Odd row class list, choose oddRow. From the Hover class list, choose hoverRow. Leave the Even row class field blank and, from the Select class list, choose selectRow.

The final operation in the Insert Spry Table dialog box is to set up the rows to update any associated Spry detail regions.

7   Check the Update detail regions when row is clicked option; click OK when you're done. When Dreamweaver asks if you'd like to add a Spry region, click Yes.

The Spry region is a <div> tag wrapped around the table that associates the area to your previously defined data set, ds1. Let's customize the inserted table.

8   Select the column heading Company and press Delete (Windows) or forward delete (MacOS); enter **Client** as the new column header. Select the column heading startdate and press Delete (Windows) or forward delete (MacOS). Enter **Since** as the new column header.

9   If necessary, choose Window > Properties to display the Property inspector. From the Tag Selector, choose <table>. In the Property inspector, select dataTable from the Table Id list. In the CellSpace field, enter **0** and press Tab.

The CSS rules associated to the dataTable ID set the width for the table to 100% and add a bit of padding to all the table cells.

10   Choose File > Save. Press F12 (Windows) or Option+F12 (MacOS) to preview the page in your primary browser. Note the table of data that appears in the left column with alternating styles. Move your cursor over any of the rows to see the hover style; select a row to see the select style. Click the Since column header to change the sort order; click Company to change it back. When you're done exploring, close your browser and return to Dreamweaver.

With the master data displayed and made interactive, you're ready to move onto the detail region.

Applying Spry Detail Regions

In this exercise, you'll establish a Spry detail region that relates to the previously defined data set, ds1, and the Spry Table just inserted. Within the detail region, you'll add a dynamic image and two dynamic text elements.

1	If necessary, re-open the spry_start.htm file worked on in the previous exercise by double-clicking its entry in the Files panel.

2	Double-click the image placeholder. When the Select Image Source dialog box appears, choose the Select file name from Data sources option.

3	From the Field list, choose the pic data column. Place your cursor in the beginning of the URL field, before the data variable {ds1::pic} and enter **images/** so that the entire URL field contains images/{ds1::pic}. Click OK when you're done.

Dreamweaver displays the broken image placeholder, but don't worry: the proper image will appear when the page is viewed in the browser. Now, let's add in the dynamic text elements.

4   Select the placeholder text Description placeholder and press Delete (Windows) or forward delete (MacOS). Choose Window > Bindings. In the Behaviors panel, select desc and click Insert.

Dreamweaver inserts the code for the Spry dynamic text, {ds1::desc}, which represents both the data set, ds1, and the chosen data element, desc. Finally, let's add the second data text element.

If you only have one data set on a page, you can omit the data set reference. For example, {ds1::desc} could be written {desc}.

5   Select the placeholder text Work placeholder and press Delete (Windows) or forward delete (MacOS). From the Behaviors panel, select work and click Insert.

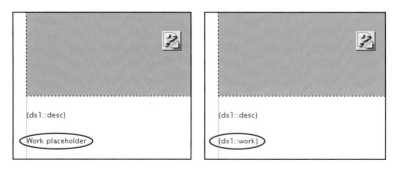

To complete the connection between the master and detail regions, you'll need to identify the Spry detail region area of the page.

6   From the Tag Selector, choose <div #rightColumn> and press Ctrl+T (Windows) or Cmd+T (MacOS). When the Quick Tag Editor appears, move your cursor between the closing quotation mark and the closing angle bracket and press Space. Enter the following code **spry:detailregion="ds1"** and press Enter (Windows) or Return (MacOS).

```
Edit tag: <div id="rightColumn"
          spry:detailregion="ds1">
```

You'll notice that the <div #rightColumn> indicator in the Tag Selector changes to a reddish-orange color; this color indicates tags with Spry attributes. In addition, because the detail region has been added, the dynamic text variables are modified to {desc} and {work}.

Note: The Quick Tag Editor offers a drop-down list of code hints that modify as you type. Once you've typed enough characters to isolate the desired attribute—for spry:detailregion, you would need to type spry:det—press Enter (Windows) or Return (MacOS) to accept the list entry. Press Enter (Windows) or Return (MacOS) again to accept the single data set.

7   Choose File > Save. Press F12 (Windows) or Option+F12 (MacOS) to preview the page in your primary browser. Select any row in the master Spry data table to change the elements in the Spry detail region. When you're done exploring, close your browser and return to Dreamweaver.

Your Spry master and detail regions are now working well together. In the next exercise, you'll add a little pizzazz to your layout with a Spry widget.

Constructing Spry Widgets

A Spry layout widget combines sophisticated JavaScript effects with integrated CSS styles to create new possibilities for Dreamweaver designers. The four Spry layout widgets are:

• Spry Menu Bar – Inserts a Web standards based navigation system with drop-down menus.

• Spry Tabbed Panels – Adds a series of containers to the page, each revealed by the click of its associated tab.

• Spry Accordion – Includes two or more collapsible panels which independently slide open when the horizontal tab is selected.

• Spry Collapsible Panel – Adds a single collapsible panel to the page that reveals or displays content interactively.

In this exercise, you'll incorporate a Spry Accordion into the Spry detail region of your layout.

Note: This exercise presents an alternative option to the design completed in the previous exercise.

1   If necessary, re-open the spry_start.htm file worked on in the previous exercise by double-clicking its entry in the Files panel.

Before you can proceed, you'll need to undo some of the changes made to the page in the previous exercises.

2   Place your cursor in the detail region content area, next to the dynamic text {work}. From the Tag Selector, select <div #rightColumn>.

3   Press Ctrl+T (Windows) or Cmd+T (MacOS). When the Quick Tag Editor appears, select the code spry:detailregion="ds1" and press Delete (Windows) or forward delete (MacOS). Press Enter (Windows) or Return (MacOS).

```
Edit tag: <div id="rightColumn">
```

Spry does not currently support nested detail regions, so you'll need to remove the Spry detail region attribute from the <div> tag surrounding the entire right column. In a later step in this exercise, you'll add the Spry detail region where needed.

4   Select both Spry dynamic text elements, {desc} and {work}, and press Delete (Windows) or forward delete (MacOS). From the Tag Selector, select the <p> tag and press Delete (Windows) or forward delete (MacOS).

Your design is now ready for the Spry Accordion panel.

5   From the Spry category of the Insert bar, click Spry Accordion (▦), the second from the right.

Dreamweaver inserts the default Spry Accordion object onto the page. The initial object includes two accordion panels with the top panel exposed; a blue tab with the label Spry Accordion: Accordion 1 and border mark the new object. Once inserted, accordion panels can be modified directly in Design view.

6   Select the placeholder phrase Label 1 and press Delete (Windows) or forward delete (MacOS); enter **About the company**. Replace the placeholder phrase Label 2 with **What we did**.

It's just as easy to modify the content as the labels with either static or dynamic content. Let's add in dynamic content from the Spry data set.

7 Select the placeholder phrase Content 1 and press Delete (Windows) or forward delete (MacOS). From the Bindings panel, select tagline and click Insert. In the Property inspector, select Heading 3 from the Format list; press Enter (Windows) or Return (MacOS). From the Bindings panel, select desc and click Insert.

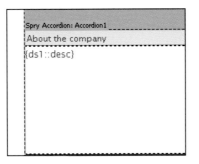

Modifying the content in an open accordion panel is very straightforward. But how do you expose a closed accordion panel for editing? Again, Dreamweaver provides a direct approach.

8 Move your cursor over the tab of the bottom accordion panel; when you see an eye icon on the right side of the tab, click the eye icon (👁). Select the placeholder phrase Content 2 and press Delete (Windows) or forward delete (MacOS). From the Bindings panel, select work and click Insert.

With all the dynamic content in place, let's reapply the Spry detail region attributes to the proper places. In all, there are three tags to modify: one for the image and one for each of the accordion panels.

9   With your cursor still in the bottom accordion panel, select <div
.AccordionPanelContent> from the Tag Selector. Press Ctrl+T (Windows) or Cmd+T
(MacOS). Once the Quick Tag Editor opens, move your cursor between the closing
quotation mark and the closing angle bracket and press Space. Enter the following code
spry:detailregion="ds1" and press Enter (Windows) or Return (MacOS).

```
Edit tag: <div
          class="AccordionPanelContent"
          spry:detailregion="ds1">
```

Let's perform the same sequence for the top accordion panel.

10   Move your cursor over the top accordion panel tab and click the Eye icon. Place
your cursor in the content area and repeat step 9 to add the spry:detailregion attribute
to the <div .AccordionPanelContent> tag for the top panel.

*Note: Make sure you select <div .AccordionPanelContent> and not <div
.AccordionPanel>. If you do not see <div .AccordionPanelContent> in the Tag Selector,
click again in the content area.*

Now, let's associate the dynamic image to same data set.

11   Select the image placeholder and, from the Tag Selector, choose <div> and press
Ctrl+T (Windows) or Cmd+T (MacOS). When the Quick Tag Editor appears, press
Space and enter the following code **spry:detailregion="ds1"**. Press Enter (Windows) or
Return (MacOS).

```
Edit tag: <div spry:detailregion="ds1">
```

All your Spry functionality is now in place—now, let's add a little CSS style.

12 Choose Window > CSS Styles. Select Attach Style Sheet (⊜) from the bottom of the CSS Styles panel. When the Attach External Style Sheet dialog box appears, click Browse. In the Select Style Sheet File dialog box, navigate to the lesson09 > css folder, select myAccordion.css and click OK (Windows) or Choose (MacOS). Leave the other settings at their default and click OK.

The external CSS file includes several rules that change the accordion panel tab background colors and add a bit of padding to the content itself. The final touch is to reformat the accordion panel labels.

13 Place your cursor in the top accordion panel label About the company. From the Property inspector, choose Heading 3 from the Format list. Repeat this operation for the bottom accordion panel label.

The directional arrows are background images which have been applied to the h3 style; a rendering bug prevents the white arrows from appearing in Design view on the Macintosh—they will, however, appear when previewed in your browser. This page is now ready for preview and interaction.

14 Choose File > Save. When the Copy Dependent Files dialog appears, click OK. Press F12 (Windows) or Option+F12 (MacOS) to preview the page in your primary browser. Select the second data row from the master data table, Company Anon. Review the content in the top accordion panel and then click the bottom accordion panel tab to display its content. Click any other data row to reveal new images and content. When you're done, close your browser and return to Dreamweaver.

The top accordion panel shows by default.

15 Click the bottom accordion panel to see its contents.

In the next exercise, you'll take advantage of the sophisticated JavaScript functionality available in Spry effects.

Applying Spry Effects

In many ways, Spry Effects are no different from the standard behaviors covered in Lesson 08. Spry Effects are available from the Behaviors panel list, use dialog boxes to gather user-defined settings, appear in the Behaviors panel when applied, and can be easily modified at any time. There is, however, one major difference between Spry Effects and standard behaviors: Spry Effects require JavaScript functions contained in an external file. When you apply a Spry Effect, Dreamweaver automatically links to the needed JavaScript file; you'll need to be sure to post the file to your remote site when it comes time to push your site live.

In this exercise, you'll apply a Spry Effect that briefly highlights a designated element and is triggered by the loading of the page.

1   If necessary, re-open the spry_start.htm file worked on in the previous exercise by double-clicking its entry in the Files panel.

2   Place your cursor in the heading, See what we can do, and, from the Tag Selector, select <body>.

Unlike other examples covered in Lesson 08, this behavior is not triggered by a link, but rather by the page loading or, more specifically, by the onLoad event of the <body> tag.

3   Choose Window > Behaviors. In the Behaviors panel, click Add (⊞), and from the list, choose Effects > Highlight.

4   In the Highlight dialog box, choose h1 "headline" from the Target Element list. In the Effect duration field, enter **3000**. Click the End Color color swatch and, with the eyedropper tool, select the yellow color block in the second column from the left. Left the other settings at their default and click OK.

Highlight

Target Element:	h1 "headline" ▾	OK
Effect duration:	3000 milliseconds	Cancel
Start Color:	▢ #ffffff	Help
End Color:	▢ #FFFF00	
Color After Effect:	▢ #ffffff	
	☐ Toggle effect	

The Highlight behavior can be applied to almost any HTML object (except for those related to frames or the body tag itself) as long as the object has a valid ID attribute. In this example, the <h1> tag with the ID of #headline is targeted and the effect duration is set to 3 seconds with a yellow highlight.

5   In the Behaviors panel, select the newly entered behavior. Choose onLoad from the Event list adjacent to the Highlight behavior to change the event from onClick. Select the Highlight behavior and click Up (▲) to move the behavior before the Preload Images behavior.

By moving the Highlight behavior, you're setting up the behavior to trigger as soon as the rest of the page is loaded and not wait until all rollover and other initially hidden page images are preloaded.

6 Choose File > Save; after you've reviewed the information concerning the files in the Copy Dependent Files dialog box that appears, click OK. Press F12 (Windows) or Option+F12 (MacOS) to preview the page in your primary browser. Note that after the page loads, a yellow highlight fades in behind the primary headline and then, after 3 seconds, disappears. You can review this effect by clicking your browser refresh button. When you're done, close your browser and return to Dreamweaver.

The headline is automatically highlighted when the page first loads.

The highlight disappears after the specified duration.

Congratulations, you've completed this lesson!

In the next lesson, you'll learn how to incorporate forms into your Web pages.

Review

▶ Review questions

1 What does the acronym Ajax stand for and what is its primary benefit?

2 What is Spry?

3 True or False: An XML data file can only be read or written by a special program.

4 What are the four major Spry groups in Dreamweaver?

5 What is the first task in adding Spry master-detail data to your page?

6 True or False: The only way to add Spry data to the page is by hand-coding.

7 What does an accordion panel do?

8 What is the one major difference between standard Dreamweaver behaviors and Spry Effects?

▶ Review answers

1 Ajax is short for Asynchronous JavaScript and XML and is known for permitting the display of XML data as needed and refreshing only a portion of a page.

2 Spry is an Ajax framework developed by Adobe and used in Dreamweaver.

3 False: XML files are text-based and can be read and modified in any text editor, including Dreamweaver.

4 Spry Data, Spry Form widgets, Spry Layout widgets and Spry Effects.

5 The first task is to establish a connection to your XML data source known as a data set.

6 False: The Spry Table object inserts Spry data in a table format, complete with sortable columns and other advanced properties.

7   A Spry Accordion panel includes two or more collapsible panels which hide and reveal content in a contained area of the page.

8   Spry Effects require an external JavaScript file that is included whenever an Effect is applied, but must be uploaded to the remote site. With standard Dreamweaver behaviors, all the code is added to the page.

dev/design

Home Spirit Folks Work Contact

How can we help?

Request for Proposal

Your company: [   ]

Email: [   ]

Username: [   ]

Password: [   ]

Your business: [Briefly describe your
business in this space

]

Company Size: ○ Less than 10
               ○ 11 to 50
               ○ 50 to 200
               ○ Over 200

Services: ☐ Brand Identity ☐ New Website ☐ Web Redesign

Timeline: [Immediately   ▾]

[Send to dev / design]

Give us a shout

We'd love to help – all you have to do is tell us how. Lorem ipsum dolor sit amet, consetetur sadipscing elitr, sed diam nonumy eirmod tempor invidunt ut labore et dolore magna aliquyam erat, sed diam voluptua. At vero eos et accusam et justo duo dolores et ea rebum. Stet clita kasd gubergren, no sea takimata sanctus est Lorem ipsum dolor sit amet.

Lorem ipsum dolor sit amet, consetetur sadipscing elitr, sed diam nonumy eirmod tempor invidunt ut labore et dolore magna aliquyam erat, sed diam voluptua. At vero eos et accusam et justo duo dolores et ea rebum. Stet clita kasd gubergren, no sea takimata sanctus est Lorem ipsum dolor sit amet

Forms are the primary doorway for communicating with visitors to your websites. And, as with any essential element, badly implemented forms can be incredibly frustrating for both parties: the one filling out the form and the one managing the submitted data. Dreamweaver provides a robust form solution to ensure that the entering data is just as simple as receiving it.

10 | Constructing Forms

In this lesson, you'll learn how to create forms for your Web page and do the following:

- Insert a form.
- Include text fields.
- Work with Spry form widgets.
- Use radio buttons.
- Apply checkboxes.
- Insert lists.
- Add form buttons.
- Incorporate fieldsets and legends.
- Style your form with CSS.

This lesson will take about 120 minutes to complete. Be sure you have copied Lessons/Lesson10 from the Adobe Dreamweaver CS3 Classroom in a Book CD to your hard drive before beginning. As you work on this lesson, you'll overwrite the start files. If you need to restore the start files, copy them again from the CD.

Previewing your completed file

To get a sense of the file you will work on in the first part of this lesson, let's preview the completed page in the browser.

1   Start Adobe Dreamweaver CS3.

2   If necessary, press F8 to open the Files panel and choose DW CIB from the site list.

3   In the Files panel, expand the lesson10 folder.

4 Select the form_final.htm file and press F12 (Windows) or Option+F12 (MacOS) to preview it in your primary browser.

The page includes a number of different form elements.

5 If Internet Explorer is your primary browser and a message appears on top of the browser window that indicates that scripts are prevented from running, click the message bar and choose Allow Blocked Content.

6 Place your cursor in the Company field and enter a company name. Press Tab.

7 With your cursor in the Email filed, press Tab without entering an email address.

A Spry Form widget provides validation for this required field and displays an error message if the field is left empty.

8 Enter **jdoe@mycompany** and press Tab, intentionally omitting the .com portion of the email address.

The Spry Form widget ensures that the information entered is in the correct format.

9   Enter **.com** after jdoe@mycompany and press Tab.

Now that the entry is a complete email address, the error messages disappear.

10   Enter a username in the Username field with less than six characters and press Tab. Note the error message; return to the Username field and enter a username with six or more characters and press Tab. Enter a password in the Password field and press Tab.

11   Choose a size for your company from the Company Size radio buttons.

12   Select which services you'd like to request from the Services checkboxes.

13   Choose when you need your job undertaken from the Timeline list.

14   Click Send to dev / design to submit the form. Note the "thank you" page that appears in response.

Note: *No form data is actually saved.*

15   When you're done, close all browser windows and return to Dreamweaver.

Before you begin constructing your form with all the various form elements, let's take a moment to make sure you understand how forms work.

Learning about forms

Forms, whether on paper or on the Web, gather information. In both cases, each bit of information is entered in its own area to make it easier to understand the data. And, also in both cases, the form is clearly delineated: with printed forms, a separate page or border separates the form while Web forms rely on the <form> tag.

Web-based forms are composed of a series of form elements, each used for a different purpose:

• Text fields – Permit general text entry for a limited number of characters; text fields designated as password fields mask the characters as they are being input.

• Text areas – Similar to the standard text field, but intended for larger amounts of text, such as multiple sentences or paragraphs.

• Radio buttons – Displays a mutually exclusive group of options; any choice in the group replaces any previous choice.

• Checkboxes – Allows a yes or no type of selection; checkboxes can be grouped together but are not mutually exclusive.

• Lists – Displays entries in a drop-down list format. Lists (also called menus or select lists) may either permit the selection of a single element or of multiple elements.

• Hidden – Conveys information to the form processing mechanism unseen by the page visitor; hidden form elements are used extensively in dynamic page applications.

• Buttons – Used for submitting the form or performing some other interactive action, like clearing the form.

With paper, once the form has been filled out it can be mailed or handed to someone for processing. Web forms are similar, except the mailing or processing is all electronic. The <form> tag includes an action attribute; the value of the action attribute is triggered when the form is submitted. Often, the action is the Web address for another page or server-side script which actually handles the form processing.

Note: The actual processing of the form is beyond the scope of this book; this lesson describes how to set up your form in preparation for processing. To learn more about dynamic applications for storing the information in your forms, see Dreamweaver Help, "Building applications visually."

Adding a form to the page

1   From the Files panel, expand the lesson10 folder and double-click the form_start.htm file to open it.

2   Select the phrase Form placeholder and press Delete.

The form tag must surround all the form elements, so it's typically best to add it to the page first.

3   In the Insert bar, choose Forms from the category list. From the Forms category, choose Form (▢), the first icon on the left.

Dreamweaver inserts the <form> tag, indicated visually with a red dashed outline.

Note: If the outline does not appear, choose Invisible Elements from the Visual Aids menu button on the Document toolbar.

Next, you'll set the <form> tag's action attribute.

4   If necessary, choose Window > Properties to display the Property inspector. Click the folder next to the Action field. In the Select File dialog box, navigate to the lesson10 folder and select form_processing.htm; click OK (Windows) or Choose (MacOS) when you're done.

Note: You can leave the other properties at their default setting for now. The Method and Enctype attributes might be changed later, depending on the type of server side code used to process the form data. As noted earlier, this server side code would eventually be added to the page listed as the action attribute.

To give your form an overall structured appearance, let's insert a table to hold the various elements.

5   With your cursor inside the form, choose Insert > Table. In the Table dialog box, enter **9** in the Rows field and **2** in the Columns field. In the Width field, enter **100** and press Tab; from the Width list, choose percent. In the Border thickness field, enter **0**. Leave the Cell padding and Cell spacing fields blank and all the other options at their default setting. Click OK.

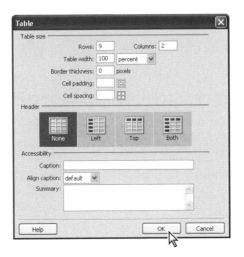

Many Web designers use a two-column table for their form elements: the left column contains the form labels, like Name and Address, while the right column holds the form elements themselves, such as text fields and checkboxes.

6   If necessary, choose Window > Properties. In the upper left corner of the Property inspector, enter **formTable** in the Name field.

Naming the table will come in handy later when you're styling your form elements.

7   Choose File > Save.

Next, you'll begin to insert your form elements, starting with the most commonly used one: text fields.

Inserting text form elements

Text fields are the real workhorse of all the form elements. As the basic tool for gathering non-structured data in short text phrases, it's hard to imagine a form without them. In fact, many forms are composed exclusively of text fields.

In the following exercises, you'll learn how to insert basic text fields, Spry Text fields, password text fields, and text areas. Before you can start, however, you'll need to make sure that Dreamweaver is ready to add form elements in their most accessible format.

Setting up for accessible forms

Form elements have special requirements when it comes to accessibility. Assistive technology like screen readers require precise code to be able to read forms and individual form elements correctly. Dreamweaver provides an option that outputs form code in the proper format.

1   Choose Edit > Preferences (Windows) or Dreamweaver > Preferences (MacOS).

2   When the Preferences dialog box appears, click Accessibility in the Category list.

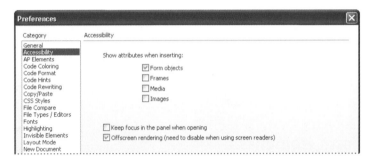

3   In the Accessibility category, make sure that the Form objects checkbox is checked and click OK.

As you'll see in the following exercises, with accessibility for form objects enabled, a dialog box appears prior to the form element being inserted. This dialog box has a number of options for including a form element label as well as other special attributes. You'll learn more about these attributes in the upcoming exercise.

Using text fields

Text fields accept alphanumeric characters—letters and numbers—for a limited number of characters. The actual physical limit for a text field is 255 characters, but most text fields are used for entering much shorter text strings, like for names or addresses.

1   If necessary, re-open the form_start.htm file worked on in the earlier exercise by double-clicking its entry in the Files panel.

2   Place your cursor in the first row of the table in the right column.

3   From the Forms category of the Insert bar, click Text field (▭), the second icon from the left.

Because you've enabled accessibility for form objects, a dialog box appears.

4   In the Input Tag Accessibility Attributes dialog box, enter **company** in the ID field and press Tab. In the Label field, enter **Company Name:** and press Tab.

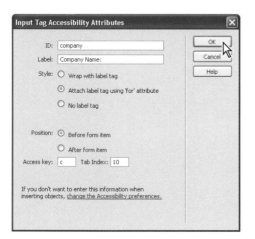

5   In the Style section, choose the Attach label tag using 'for' attribute option.

When working with a two-column table where the labels are in a separate column than the form elements always select this option rather than the Wrap with label tag option. With the Attach label tag using 'for' attribute option selected, Dreamweaver inserts code like this:

```
<label for="company">Company Name:</label><input type="text"
id="company" />
```

This code arrangement allows the <label> tag to be completely separated from the form element <input> tag, in two separate table cells.

6   Make sure that the Position: Before form item option is selected. In the Access key field, enter **c** and press Tab. In the Tab Index field, enter **10**. Click OK when you're done.

💡 *Labels for text fields are, typically, placed before the field itself; this setting, however, is irrelevant since you'll be moving the labels in just a moment.*

The Access key field defines which key, when pressed in combination with the browser's modifier, gives focus to that field. For example, if a page visitor using Internet Explorer (version 6 or higher) presses Alt+c while browsing this page, the company field would be selected and ready for input. You'll be assigning individual access keys for all the form elements on this page.

Note: The access modifier for Firefox is Shift+Alt and for Safari, it is the Control key.

The Tab Index is another accessibility aid. The Tab Index determines the order in which the various form fields receive focus when the Tab key is pressed. The lowest number on the page is the first to receive focus, followed by the next highest number and so on.

💡 *It's a good idea to initially enter Tab Index values in a multiple of ten (10, 20, 30, etc.) to allow for other form fields to be inserted later without renumbering the entire form.*

7   Place your cursor in the text Company Name and, from the Tag Selector, choose <label>. Drag the selection to the first table column in the same row.

8   Choose File > Save.

The first of your form objects is now in place. Inserting other standard text fields is a similar operation. In the next exercise, you'll learn how to add a specialized version of the text field, Dreamweaver's Spry Text field.

Including Spry Text fields

In Lesson 08, you learned about Dreamweaver's Ajax framework, Spry, and worked with a number of the Spry tools, like Spry Data and the Spry Accordion Panel. Dreamweaver also includes a range of Spry objects for forms. Each Spry Form widget combines form elements with sophisticated JavaScript to create easy-to-use form objects with built-in validation.

Validation is the process of verifying that the proper data has been entered into a particular form element. For example, if the site visitor entered an incomplete or invalid email address into an email text field, the data would be worthless. Validation can also ensure that required form fields are completed before the form can be submitted.

There are Spry Form widgets for four different form elements: text fields, text areas, checkboxes and select lists. Each widget works basically the same way: you insert the object and then adjust the properties through the Property inspector. In this exercise, you'll insert a Spry Validation Text Field object to make sure your form submits properly formatted email addresses.

1   If necessary, re-open the form_start.htm file worked on in the earlier exercise by double-clicking its entry in the Files panel.

2   From the Forms category of the Insert bar, drag the Spry Validation Text Field (▣) object, the fourth icon from the right, to the right column in the second row.

3   In the Input Tag Accessibility Attributes dialog box, enter **email** in the ID field and press Tab. In the Label field, enter **Email:** and press Tab. In the Style section, make sure that choose the Attach label tag using 'for' attribute option is selected. In the Access key field, enter **e** and press Tab. In the Tab Index field, enter **20**. Click OK when you're done.

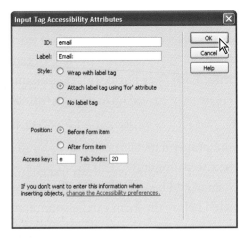

4   Choose File > Save. When Dreamweaver alerts you of the external JavaScript files used, click OK.

Now that our form element is on the page—with the added Spry functionality—let's begin to customize it, starting with the label placement.

5   Place your cursor in the text Email and, from the Tag Selector, choose <label>. Drag the selection to the first table column in the same row.

Next, let's specify the type of validation.

6   Move your cursor over the email text field until the Spry Textfield tab appears; click the tab to select the object.

The custom Property inspector provides a lot of information and adjustable attributes.

7   If necessary, choose Window > Properties to display the Property inspector. From the Type list, choose Email Address.

As you can see there are a large number of validation types to choose from, including everything from Integer to Custom. The Email Address validation makes sure that the entry contains an @ character which is followed by a domain name. Now, let's set up the validation trigger.

8   In the Property inspector, choose the Validate on Blur option and make sure that the Required option is selected.

By default, all validations are triggered when the form is submitted. In most cases, you can add additional triggers. Here, the field is checked for an entry with a proper email format after the site visitor has tabbed or clicked away from the field. This provides a more immediate reaction and better user experience. If the field is skipped altogether, the Required option ensures that an error message will be displayed when the form is submitted. Now, let's customize that error message.

9   From the Preview states list, choose Required. Select the default error text next to the field, A value is required, and press Delete. Enter **Required**.

Now, whenever this form is submitted without any entry whatsoever in the email field, the Required error is shown. Next, let's customize the error message that appears if an invalid email address is entered.

10   Move your cursor over the email text field until the Spry Textfield tab appears; click the tab to select the object. In the Property inspector, choose Invalid Format from the Preview states list. Select the default error text, Invalid Format, and press Delete (Windows) or forward delete (MacOS). Enter **Full email address**.

Some text fields don't require a particular format, but may need a certain number of characters to be entered. In the next series of steps, you'll add a Spry Text field to the page that has a minimum character requirement.

11   From the Forms category of the Insert bar, drag the Spry Validation Text Field object to the right column in the third row.

12   In the Input Tag Accessibility Attributes dialog box, enter **username** in the ID field and press Tab. In the Label field, enter **Username:** and press Tab. In the Style section, make sure that choose the Attach label tag using 'for' attribute option is selected. In the Access key field, enter **u** and press Tab. In the Tab Index field, enter **30**. Click OK when you're done.

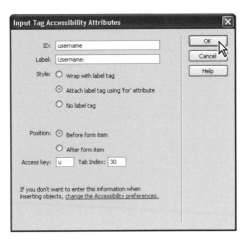

13 Place your cursor in the text Username and, from the Tag Selector, choose <label>. Drag the selection to the first column in the same row.

14 Move your cursor over the username text field until the Spry Textfield tab appears; click the tab to select the object.

15 In the Property inspector, select the Validate on Blur option and enter **6** in the Min Chars field and press Tab.

Dreamweaver displays a new preview state and accompanying error message. Let's tighten up that message a bit.

16 Select the default error message, Minimum number of characters not met, and press Delete (Windows) or forward delete (MacOS). Enter **6 or more characters**.

Finally, let's customize the required error message as before.

17 Move your cursor over the username text field until the Spry Textfield tab appears; click the tab to select the object. From the Preview states list of the Property inspector, choose Required. Select the default error text next to the field, A value is required, and press Delete (Windows) or forward delete (MacOS). Enter **Required**.

18 Choose File > Save.

The form is beginning to take shape! In the next exercise, you'll enter another type of text field, the password field.

Applying password fields

The password field is a common sight on the Web. Normally, a text field displays the characters entered into it. However, when the text field is turned into a password field, the characters entered are masked and depicted as a series of asterisks or bullets, depending on the browser.

1   If necessary, re-open the form_start.htm file worked on in the earlier exercise by double-clicking its entry in the Files panel.

2   From the Forms category of the Insert bar, drag the Text Field object, to the right column in the fourth row.

3   In the Input Tag Accessibility Attributes dialog box, enter **password** in the ID field and press Tab. In the Label field, enter **Password:** and press Tab. In the Style section, make sure that choose the Attach label tag using 'for' attribute option is selected. In the Access key field, enter **p** and press Tab. In the Tab Index field, enter **40**. Click OK when you're done.

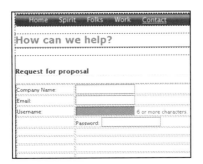

4   Place your cursor in the text Password and, from the Tag Selector, choose <label>. Drag the selection to the first column in the same row.

Now let's turn the standard text field into a password field.

5   Select the password text field. In the Property inspector, select the Password option.

The change won't be apparent until you test your page in the browser and enter any characters into this field.

6   Choose File > Save.

In the next exercise, you'll add a form element better suited to large amounts of text, a text area.

Incorporating text areas

Text areas allow for a greater amount of text to be entered than text fields. Text areas permit multiple line entry and, by default, word wrapping. If the entered text exceeds the physical space of the text area on the page, scroll bars automatically appear to allow the overflow text to be read.

1   If necessary, re-open the form_start.htm file worked on in the earlier exercise by double-clicking its entry in the Files panel.

2   From the Forms category of the Insert bar, drag Text Area (▣), the fourth icon from the left, to the right column in the fifth row.

3   In the Input Tag Accessibility Attributes dialog box, enter **business** in the ID field and press Tab. In the Label field, enter **Your Business:** and press Tab. In the Style section, make sure that choose the Attach label tag using 'for' attribute option is selected. In the Access key field, enter **b** and press Tab. In the Tab Index field, enter **50**. Click OK when you're done.

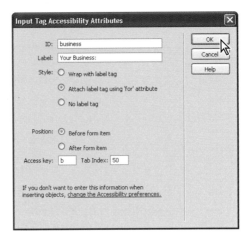

4   Place your cursor in the text Your Business and, from the Tag Selector, choose <label>. Drag the selection to the first column in the same row.

The label appears in the vertical middle of the row due to the height of the text area. You'll adjust this appearance in a later exercise through CSS styling.

5   Select the business text area. In the Property inspector, enter **Briefly describe your business in this space** in the Init val field and press Tab.

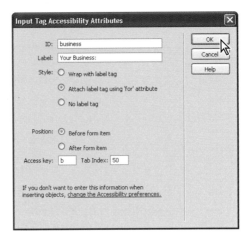

It's often a good idea to use the Init val field (short for Initial Value) to display a helpful message to describe what is expected in a particular form element.

6 Choose File > Save.

In the next exercise, you'll learn how to offer mutually exclusive options on your form with radio buttons.

Including radio buttons

When you want people to choose one from a number of items offered, you use a group of radio buttons. Unlike other form elements, each radio button does not have a unique name; rather, all radio buttons in the same group have the same name. To differentiate between radio buttons, each is given a distinctive value.

Dreamweaver provides two methods for adding radio buttons to your page. You can either individually insert each radio button or insert an entire group at once. Each technique has its pros and cons. If you insert the radio buttons separately, you'll need to rename each of them to ensure that they all have the same name. If you add them as a group, they will all have the same name, but you'll need to add accessibility attributes to each. The following exercise takes the latter approach to reinforce the radio button group concept and to reveal the code used to add an access key and tab index to a form element.

1 If necessary, re-open the form_start.htm file worked on in the earlier exercise by double-clicking its entry in the Files panel.

2 From the Forms category of the Insert bar, drag Radio Group (▤), the seventh icon from the left, to the right column in the sixth row.

3 In the Radio Group dialog box, enter **size** in the Name field.

4 This group of radio buttons will be used to assess the size of the company submitting the form.

5 Select the first entry in the Label column. Enter **Less than 10** and press Tab; when the entry in the Value column is selected, enter **less10**. Press Tab again to move to the second row. Enter **10 to 50** and press Tab; in the Value column enter **10to50**.

Each row creates a new radio button. However, you're not limited to two radio buttons—let's add a couple more.

6 Click Add to insert a new row. Select the new entry in the Label column and enter **50 to 200** as a new label; press Tab and enter **50to200** as the value. Click Add to insert a final new row. Select the new entry in the Label column and enter **Over 200**; press Tab one last time and enter **over200**.

Because you're adding multiple radio buttons at that same time, Dreamweaver offers your choice for their layout. To avoid nested tables, let's go with separating each with a line break.

7 Make sure that the Lay out using option is set to Line breaks (
 tags) and click OK.

When the radio group is inserted you'll notice that, unlike with other form elements, there is no overall label to place in the first column. Let's do that now.

💡 *You can enable any radio button in a group to be the default choice by choosing that radio button and, in the Property inspector, selecting the Initial State to be Checked. In this scenario, none of the radio buttons are selected because there is no way of knowing the company size.*

8   Place your cursor in the first column on the same row as the radio group and enter **Company Size:**.

The final task in this exercise is to add the accessibility attributes to the newly inserted radio buttons.

9   Select the first radio button and press Ctrl+T (Windows) or Cmd+T (MacOS) to open the Quick Tag Editor. Place your cursor before the closing two characters, **/>**, and enter **accesskey="1" tabindex="60"**. Press Enter (Windows) or Return (MacOS).

Note: *The accesskey for the first radio button is a lowercase L (as in Less than 10) whereas the accesskey for the second radio button will be the number 1.*

10 Repeat step 11 for each of the remaining three radio buttons and enter the following code in sequence:

- **accesskey="1" tabindex="70"**
- **accesskey="5" tabindex="80"**
- **accesskey="o" tabindex="90"**

11 Choose File > Save.

Next, you'll learn how to offer choices that are not mutually exclusive with checkboxes.

Inserting checkboxes

Checkboxes provide a series of options which can be selected in any combination. Each checkbox has its own name and value that is submitted if the form element is checked. Unlike radio buttons, checkboxes can only be inserted one at a time.

1 If necessary, re-open the form_start.htm file worked on in the earlier exercise by double-clicking its entry in the Files panel.

2 From the Forms category of the Insert bar, drag Checkbox (☑), the fifth icon from the left, to the right column in the seventh row.

3   In the Input Tag Accessibility Attributes dialog box, enter **identity** in the ID field and press Tab. In the Label field, enter **Brand Identity** and press Tab. In the Style section, make sure that choose the Attach label tag using 'for' attribute option is selected. Make sure that Position is set to After form item. In the Access key field, enter **i** and press Tab. In the Tab Index field, enter **100**. Click OK when you're done.

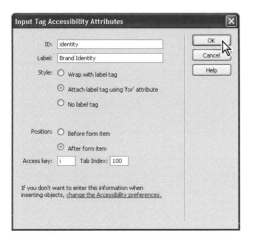

Now, let's position our cursor to insert another checkbox.

4   Place your cursor after the label Brand Identity and, from the Tag Selector, choose <label>. Press right arrow to move your cursor outside of the selected tag. Press Space.

5   Repeat steps 3 and 4 to add two more checkboxes with these values:

- ID: **newweb**; Label: **New Website**; Access key: **n**; and Tab Index: **110**

- ID: **redesign**; Label: **Web Redesign**; Access key: **w**; and Tab Index: **120**

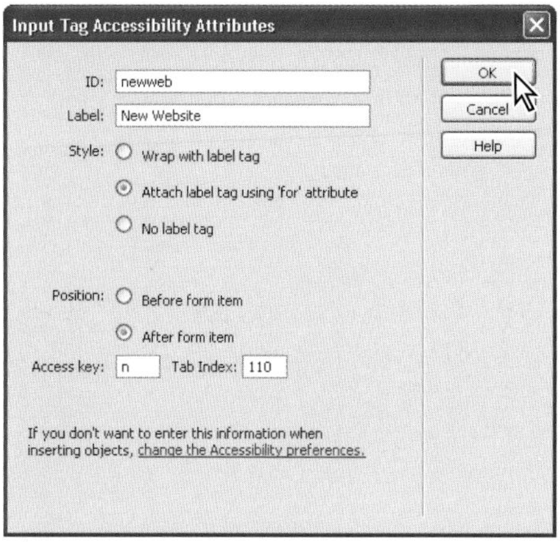

Second checkbox attributes

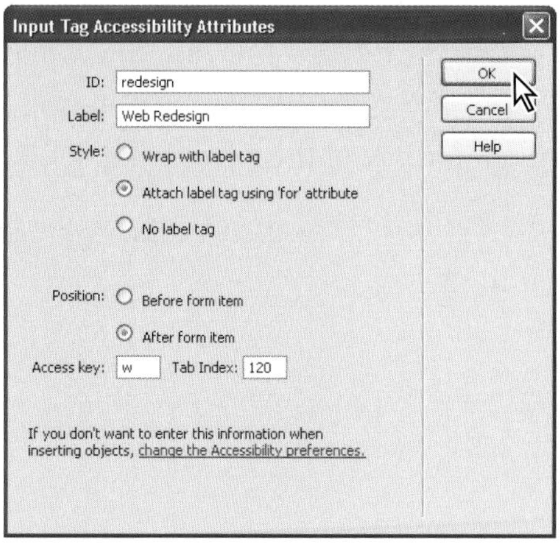

Third checkbox attributes

6   Place your cursor in the first column on the same row as the checkboxes and enter **Services:**.

7 Choose File > Save.

Next, you'll learn how to present multiple choices in a more compact format with the list form element.

Working with lists

Drop-down list form elements are a flexible method of presenting multiple options. The standard list offers a single, mutually exclusive choice, like a radio button group. However, when the multiple selection option is enabled, the list behaves more like a series of checkboxes. In this exercise, you'll insert a standard list with three options.

1 If necessary, re-open the form_start.htm file worked on in the earlier exercise by double-clicking its entry in the Files panel.

2 From the Forms category of the Insert bar, drag List/Menu (▤), the eighth icon from the left, to the right column in the eighth row.

3 In the Input Tag Accessibility Attributes dialog box, enter **timeline** in the ID field and press Tab. In the Label field, enter **Timeline:** and press Tab. In the Style section, make sure that choose the Attach label tag using 'for' attribute option is selected. Make sure that Position is set to Before form item. In the Access key field, enter **t** and press Tab. In the Tab Index field, enter **130**. Click OK when you're done.

4 Place your cursor in the text Timeline and, from the Tag Selector, choose <label>. Drag the selection to the first column in the same row.

5 Now you're ready to add the list entries. Dreamweaver provides a separate dialog box for this task, accessible through the Property inspector.

6 Select the list form element just inserted. If necessary, choose Window > Properties. Click List Values.

7   In the List Values dialog box, click Add. In the Item Label column, enter
Immediately and press Tab. Enter **now** in the Value column. Press Tab.

Like a table, pressing Tab when your cursor is in the last entry creates a new row for
additional entries.

8   Repeat step 7 to add two more list entries:

- Item Label: **In the next 2 months**; Value: **2months**

- Item Label: **Sometime this year**; Value: **year**

9   Click OK when you're done.

Now let's set the list element we want display when the page loads; typically, this is the
first item in the list.

10   In the Property inspector, select Immediately in the Initially selected list.

11   Choose File > Save.

Your form is almost complete—the last key step is to add a button to submit all the
entered information.

Adding a submit button to a form

In some ways, the submit button is the pièce de résistance of a form. As the name implies, this form object submits the entire form for processing and thus, is an essential element. By default, the button object in Dreamweaver is set to submit although other options are available. You could, for example, include a button to reset the form.

1   If necessary, re-open the form_start.htm file worked on in the earlier exercise by double-clicking its entry in the Files panel.

2   From the Forms category of the Insert bar, drag Button (▣), the seventh icon from the right, to the right column in the final row.

3   In the Input Tag Accessibility Attributes dialog box, enter **submit** in the ID field and press Tab. In the Label field, enter **Send to dev / design** and press Tab. In the Style section, choose Attach label using 'for' attribute.. In the Access key field, enter **s** and press Tab. In the Tab Index field, enter **140**. Click OK when you're done.

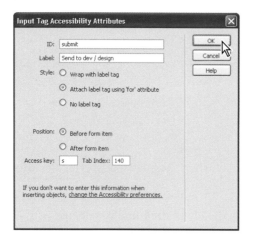

With buttons, there is no external label: the label should appear on the button itself. Unfortunately, Dreamweaver treats buttons like other form elements and adds the label text to the left. You'll need to move it to achieve the desired effect.

4   Select the label text Send to dev / design and press Ctrl+X (Windows) or Cmd+X (MacOS). From the Property inspector, select Submit in the Value field and press Delete (Windows) or forward delete (MacOS). Press Ctrl+V (Windows) or Cmd+V (MacOS) to insert the cut text; press Tab to confirm the change.

5   Choose File > Save.

All the form elements are now in place and it's time to add some stylistic flair to your form in the next exercise.

Styling your forms

While the form you've been working on in this lesson is now functional, it is completely unstyled. A well-styled form brings enhanced readability and comprehension and, is therefore easier to use. In the following exercises, you'll add style to your form in two ways: first, by grouping the form structurally and second, through the power of CSS.

Framing with fieldset and legend

The <fieldset> and <legend> tags are used together to group form elements. The <fieldset> tag places a border around the group, while <legend> adds a text header in the upper left of the <legend> border. In this exercise, you'll use these two tags to replace the current header and give the form a cohesive look-and-feel.

1   If necessary, re-open the form_start.htm file worked on in the earlier exercise by double-clicking its entry in the Files panel.

2   Place your cursor in the current header above the form, Request for Proposal. In the Tag Selector, select <h2> and press Delete (Windows) or forward delete (MacOS).

Now, let's select the element we want to wrap the <fieldset> tag around: the <table>.

3 Place your cursor anywhere in the table containing the form elements. In the Tag Selector, select <table#formTable >.

4 From the Forms category of the Insert bar, click Fieldset (▭), the fifth icon from the right.

5 When the Fieldset dialog box appears, enter **Request for Proposal** in the Legend field; click OK.

Dreamweaver wraps the entire table with a thin border with the legend in the upper left corner.

6 To see the full effect of the added fieldset and legend, choose Hide All Visual Aids from the Visual Aids menu button of the Document toolbar. When you're finished, choose it again to restore the visual aids.

7 Choose File > Save.

The final task for this page is to apply the desired CSS styles.

Applying CSS rules

Even though there are a wide range of different types of form elements, they all share certain common characteristics—a great benefit when it comes to styling them. Another benefit of styling forms, especially forms in tables, is that they are well-structured. This structure makes it possible to do a lot of styling with just a few CSS rules.

1   If necessary, re-open the form_start.htm file worked on in the earlier exercise by double-clicking its entry in the Files panel.

2   Choose Window > CSS Styles.

To save you the chore of defining all the needed styles, they're all defined for you in an external style sheet; all you need do is attach it.

3   In the CSS Styles panel, click Attach Style Sheet (⊕) at the bottom of the panel.

4   When the Attach Style Sheet dialog box appears, click Browse. Navigate to the lesson10 > css folder and select form.css; click OK (Windows) or Choose (MacOS). Leave the other settings at their default and click OK.

Two major changes are apparent. First, the contents of the <legend> tag are now bolder, larger and blue-colored tag. Second, the padding has increased between the table rows; this occurred because you gave the table a name of formTable when the table was first inserted and a couple of the CSS rules use this selector. The other CSS rules in the external style sheet are defined as classes and must be applied manually.

5   Place your cursor in the first cell of the table which contains the label Company Name: and drag down to the last cell with the label Timeline: so that all label cells are selected.

6   If necessary, choose Window > Properties. In the Property inspector, choose formLabel from the Style list.

All the labels are now bolded and aligned to the right of their respective table cells. You'll need to apply a different class to two of the cells, however, to get the desired look.

7   Select the two label cells Your Business: and Company Size: and, from the Style list, choose formLabelTop.

With all labels properly aligned, both horizontally and vertically, you're ready to standardize the widths of other fields by selectively applying a CSS class.

8   Select the company text field and, from the Class list of the Property inspector, choose inputField.

Repeat step 8 for the email, username, and password text fields as well as for the business text area and the timeline list.

Note: Make sure you've correctly selected the two fields (email and username) inside the Spry Textfields and not the Spry Textfields themselves.

Now that all your fields are aligned by width, your form is completely styled. Let's save it and take it for a test drive!

10 Choose File > Save. Press F12 (Windows) or Option+F12 (MacOS) to preview the page in your primary browser. Enter **data** in the form to try out the various validation routines in the email and username field. When you've filled out the form, click Send to dev / design and confirm that the "thank you" page appears. When you're done, close your browser and return to Dreamweaver.

Congratulations, you've completed this lesson!

Review

▶ Review questions

1   What is the purpose of the <form> tag?

2   How do you enable the accessibility features for forms in Dreamweaver?

3   Name two accessibility features available to form objects. What do they do?

4   What advantage does the Spry Form widget have over standard form objects?

5   What's the difference between a standard text field and a text area?

6   How do you designate that separate radio buttons belong to a group?

7   What's the main difference between radio buttons and checkboxes?

8   What does a <fieldset> tag do?

▶ Review answers

1   The <form> tag wraps around all the form elements (and the table that contains them) and includes an action attribute which defines the file or script to handle the form processing.

2   In Dreamweaver Preferences, under the Accessibility category, make sure Form Objects are selected.

3   Access key and Tab index. An access key defines a single letter that, when pressed in conjunction with the browser's modifier, gives focus to the associated field. The tab index indicates the order for tabbing from one field to the next.

4   Spry Form widgets include built-in validation to ensure that the data submitted is properly formed and available, if required.

5   A standard text field is intended for short characters strings, while a text area can hold multiple paragraphs.

6   All radio buttons with the same name will be in the same radio button group.

7 Radio buttons only allow for mutually exclusive choices while checkboxes permit the user to choose as many as desired.

8 A <fieldset> tag is used to group related form fields with a border; the accompanying <legend> tag identifies the group.

dev/design

Home Spirit Folks <u>Work</u> Contact

Can we give you a lift...

Media made simple

Like a stroll through the park

Lorem ipsum dolor sit amet, consetetur sadipscing elitr, sed diam nonumy eirmod tempor invidunt ut labore et dolore magna aliquyam erat, sed diam voluptua. At vero eos et accusam et justo duo dolores et ea rebum. Stet clita kasd gubergren, no sea takimata sanctus est Lorem ipsum dolor sit amet.

No cliches allowed

Lorem ipsum dolor sit amet, consetetur sadipscing elitr, sed diam nonumy eirmod tempor invidunt ut labore et dolore magna aliquyam erat, sed diam voluptua.

Interactivity re-defined

Lorem ipsum dolor sit amet, consetetur sadipscing elitr, sed diam nonumy eirmod tempor invidunt ut labore et dolore magna aliquyam erat, sed diam voluptua. At vero eos et accusam et justo duo dolores et ea rebum. Stet clita kasd gubergren, no sea takimata sanctus est Lorem ipsum dolor sit amet.

Lorem ipsum dolor sit amet, consetetur sadipscing elitr, sed diam nonumy eirmod tempor invidunt ut labore et dolore magna aliquyam erat, sed diam voluptua. At vero eos et accusam et justo duo dolores et ea rebum. Stet clita kasd gubergren, no sea takimata sanctus est Lorem ipsum dolor sit amet.

The ultimate wishlist

| Reach for your goals | 1 | of 3 | ◄◄ | ► | ►► |

Some people want their own plane

© 2007 dev/design LLC.

Want to make a Web page come to life? Add one or more multimedia elements to the mix. Today, Web multimedia means Flash: Flash movies, Flash video and even Flash slide shows. Master the techniques for incorporating any or all of these different media types into your pages and watch your visitors multiply: the true meaning of "multi" media.

11 Adding Multimedia

In this lesson, you'll learn how to incorporate a range of multimedia into your Web page and do the following:

- Insert a Flash movie.
- Add a Flash video.
- Create a Flash slide show.

This lesson will take about 60 minutes to complete. Be sure you have copied Lessons/Lesson11 from the Adobe Dreamweaver CS3 Classroom in a Book CD to your hard drive before beginning. As you work on this lesson, you'll overwrite the start files. If you need to restore the start files, copy them again from the CD.

Previewing your completed file

To get a sense of the file you will work on in the first part of this lesson, let's preview the completed page in the browser.

1   Start Adobe Dreamweaver CS3.

2   If necessary, press F8 to open the Files panel and choose DW CIB from the site list.

3   In the Files panel, expand the lesson11 folder.

4   Select the media_final.htm file and press F12 (Windows) or Option+F12 (MacOS) to preview it in your primary browser.

The page includes a number of different media elements.

5   If Internet Explorer is your primary browser and a message appears on top of the browser window that indicates that JavaScript are prevented from running, click the message bar and choose Allow Blocked Content.

6   Note that the Flash movie plays immediately when the page loads.

7   Move your cursor over the video in the left column and click Play to watch the Flash video. Experiment with the other video controls, including dragging the playhead to various parts of the video.

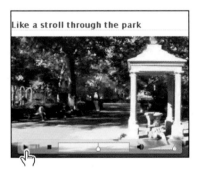

You'll notice that if you move your cursor away from the video the controls fade away—and return when your cursor is over the video.

8   In the lower right column, click Play to view the embedded slide show. Note the changing captions and transitions.

9   When you're done, close all browser windows and return to Dreamweaver.

As you can see, Dreamweaver offers a wide range of different multimedia opportunities. Let's start by adding an animated Flash movie to the page.

Placing a Flash movie on the Web

Adobe Flash is multimedia defined. From its humble beginnings as an animation program, Flash has grown rapidly to handle top-line advertisements, user interfaces and even video. As befits this highly versatile authoring tool, the tool required for playing back the output SWF files, the Flash Player, enjoys the widest distribution of any browser plug in.

Dreamweaver provides seamless integration with Flash movies. Easily inserted, SWF files are instantly previewable in the Document window. Moreover, key properties, such as Autoplay and Loop, are quickly modified through the Property inspector. If the Flash movie source file is available, you can even send the SWF to Flash for editing and automatically re-export it to return it to Dreamweaver.

In this exercise, you'll insert a basic Flash movie in the header area of your Web page. Before you can begin work on the page itself, let's be sure a pair of essential settings is enabled.

1 Choose Edit > Preferences (Windows) or Dreamweaver > Preferences (MacOS).

2 When the Preferences dialog box opens, click Code Rewriting in the Category list.

3 In the Active Content area, make sure that both options—Insert using browser-safe scripts and Convert tags to scripts on file open—are checked. Click OK.

With both options selected, Dreamweaver inserts code designed to handle Internet Explorer active content security measures unobtrusively. The first option ensures that the code is applied whenever a new Flash movie (or SWF file) is added to the page while the second option offers to rewrite older code when pages which include one or more SWF movies are opened for editing in Dreamweaver.

Note: To learn more about the issues of working with active content in Internet Explorer and the Adobe solution, visit http://www.adobe.com/devnet/activecontent/.

4 From the Files panel, expand the lesson11 folder and double-click the media_start. htm file to open it.

Dreamweaver's placeholder image capabilities are used to reserve space for the various media elements inserted during this lesson.

5 Select the placeholder image Flash_FMA and press Delete (Windows) or forward delete (MacOS).

💡 *FMA is a marketing industry abbreviation for Flexible Marketing Area.*

6 From the Common category of the Insert bar, choose Flash (🅕) under the Media menu button.

7 When the Select File dialog box appears, navigate to the lesson11 > assets folder and select fma_lift.swf; click OK (Windows) or Choose (MacOS).

Dreamweaver inserts the Flash code, represented by a placeholder element in Design view. As noted earlier, you can preview your newly inserted Flash movie right in Dreamweaver.

8 If necessary, choose Window > Properties. In the Property inspector, click Play.

By default, the SWF file plays repeatedly. However, in this situation, the Flash movie is designed to only be played once, so you'll need to set that attribute next.

9 In the Property inspector, click Stop. Uncheck the Loop checkbox and make sure to leave the Autoplay option checked.

Your Flash movie is now ready to go. However, Dreamweaver has one more bit of information to impart.

10 Choose File > Save. After the file is stored, Dreamweaver informs you that a JavaScript file, AC_RunActiveContent.js, is needed by the Flash movie and must be transferred to your remote site when the page is published to the Web. Click Okay.

Next, you'll bring a Flash video onto your page.

Showing Flash video

Because the Flash Player is almost universally available in current browsers, the introduction of Flash video was revolutionary. Overnight, all the hassles and confusion about incompatible video formats and players vanished. With each subsequent release of the Flash Player, the quality of the video—along with the ubiquity of its use—has increased; Flash video is now the leading video presentation format on the Web.

A native Flash video file has a FLV file extension and can be played in one of two ways:

• Progressive Download – Begins playing after a brief delay as soon as the first segment has been received by the browser; it continues to download while the video plays. Progressive download FLV files can be hosted on any standard Web server.

• Streaming – Starts playing immediately and offers other advantages, such as seekability, which means the video playhead can be moved to any position to begin playing at that point instantly, over the progressive download format. However, streaming FLV files must be hosted on a specialized Web server such as Flash Media Server.

In this exercise, you'll add an FLV in progressive download format to your page.

1   If necessary, re-open the media_start.htm file worked on in the earlier exercise by double-clicking its entry in the Files panel.

2   Select the image placeholder Flash_Video and press Delete (Windows) or forward delete (MacOS).

Like a stroll through the park

Flash_Video (360 x 240)

3   From the Common category of the Insert bar, choose Flash Video ( ) from the Media menu button.

4   When the Insert Flash Video dialog box appears, make sure Video Type is set to Progressive Download Video. Click Browse and in the Select Flash Video dialog, navigate to the lesson11 > assets folder and choose realty_park.flv; click OK (Windows) or Choose (MacOS).

Note: If you ever have occasion to work with streaming video, you'll notice a different set of options after selecting that video type.

The video controls are maintained in a separate file known as a skin. Dreamweaver includes nine different skins to choose from. Let's select one that overlays the video and appears only when the site visitor's mouse is over the video.

5 From the Skin list, choose Corona Skin 3. Note that the minimum width of the video is indicated for each skin. Verify that the selected FLV file meets the minimum width requirement by clicking Detect Size.

Once the size is detected, the combined size of the skin and video are displayed. Because the current skin selection appears over the video, the total size is unchanged.

6 Make sure that neither the Auto play nor Auto rewind options are selected. Leave the default message that appears if the user does not have the proper version of the Flash Player installed and click OK.

As with the SWF file, Dreamweaver inserts a placeholder with a custom Property inspector. Unlike Flash movies, however, Flash video cannot be previewed within Dreamweaver and must be viewed in a browser.

7 Choose File > Save and press F12 (Windows) or Option+F12 (MacOS) to preview the page in your primary browser. After the video loads, move your cursor over the still image to reveal the player controls. Press Play to verify the movie is working correctly. When you're done, close your browser and return to Dreamweaver.

Next, you'll add a Flash slide show, complete with smooth transitions.

Integrating a Flash slide show

Slide shows are a great way to present a series of images in a contained space. The more sophisticated slide shows, like the one you'll apply in this exercise, offer transitions, captions and separate links for each image. Best of all, this Flash movie is completely customizable.

The tool used to create the slide show is called the Image Viewer. The Image Viewer is a special type of Flash output called a Flash element. Flash elements work differently—and are applied differently—than standard Flash movies. The process for including a Flash element takes three steps:

• First, you insert the Flash element object onto the page from the Insert > Media menu.

• Next, you save an instance (or copy) of the Flash element as a SWF file in your site.

• Finally, you configure the various Flash element properties through a custom Dreamweaver panel.

Each Flash element is unique in its number and type of properties available; the Image Viewer, for example, offers 20 different user-definable options. Let's get started!

1   If necessary, re-open the media_start.htm file worked on in the earlier exercise by double-clicking its entry in the Files panel.

2   Select the image placeholder Flash_Slide_Show and press Delete (Windows) or forward delete (MacOS).

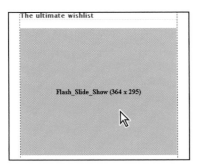

3   Choose Insert > Media > Image Viewer.

4   When the Save Flash Element dialog box appears, navigate to the lesson11 > assets folder and, in the File name field, enter **slideshow.swf**. Click OK (Windows) or Save (MacOS) when you're done.

The Flash elements panel appears with its list of properties; before you start modifying those, let's handle a more immediate issue. By default, the Image Viewer is 400 pixels wide and 325 pixels high. This width is too large for the current layout and the placeholder is forced to the bottom of the page. Luckily, you can easily resize it to make it fit your design.

5   If necessary, choose Window > Properties to display the Property inspector. In the Width field, enter **364** and press Tab. In the Height field, enter **295** and press Tab.

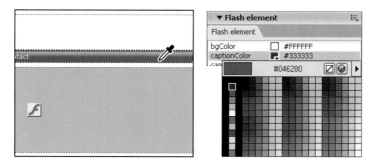

The movie resizes and now works within the layout. Now, let's begin to set the parameters for your slide show, starting with the color scheme.

6   In the Flash elements panel, select the captionColor color swatch. With the Eyedropper tool, sample the dark blue color at very bottom of the navigation bar.

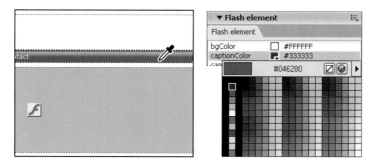

By sampling colors from your layout, you begin to incorporate the image viewer into your page; the resulting color should be #046280. Once you've identified one color, it's easy to apply that color to other properties.

7   Click the frameColor color swatch and use the Eyedropper tool to sample the captionColor color swatch. Repeat this process for the titleColor property. If your Flash element panel is too near the bottom border, the color picker will obscure the

upper colors when opened; reposition the panel a bit higher to access the proper color swatches.

Let's continue the customization by specifying new font sizes.

8   Change the captionSize value from 10 to **14** and press Tab. Repeat this change for the titleSize value so that both are **14**.

Flash element	
bgColor	☐ #FFFFFF
captionColor	■ #046280
captionFont	Verdana
captionSize	14
frameColor	■ #046280
frameShow	(No)
frameThickness	2
imageCaptions	[]
imageLinks	['http://macromedia.com…
imageLinkTarget	_blank
imageURLs	['img1.jpg','img2.jpg','img…
showControls	(Yes)
slideAutoPlay	(No)
slideDelay	5
slideLoop	(No)
title	
titleColor	■ #046280
titleFont	Verdana
titleSize	14
transitionsType	Random

Some Flash elements properties, like frameShow, use lists to present a limited number of options.

9   From the list next to frameShow, choose (Yes).

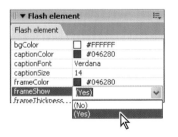

Other properties, like imageCaptions and imageLinks, must be able to accept multiple values; these values are stored in an array. Flash elements rely on a special dialog box to accept these array values. Let's see how they work.

10 Click the value field next to imageCaptions and then click Edit (📝), the icon on the far right of the field. When the Edit "imageCaptions" Array dialog appears, click in the first field under Value and enter **Some people want their own plane** and press Tab. Enter the second caption, **Other folks want to fly off a mountain** and press Tab. Enter the final caption, **While others crave the city life** and click OK.

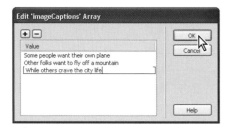

Now, let's use a similar procedure to provide links from the images that go with these captions.

💡 *It's a good idea to always include links from the slide images. If none are provided, the default links go to Adobe.com, which may not be the desired location.*

11 Click the value field next to imageLinks and then click Edit. When the Edit "imageLinks" Array dialog appears, click in the first field under Value and then click the folder icon. In the Select File dialog box, navigate to the lesson11 > images folder and select airplane_large.jpg; click OK (Windows) or Choose (MacOS). Click the second field and repeat this procedure to select snowboarder_large.jpg. Repeat the process a third time for the third field and select city_large.jpg. Click OK when you're done.

Now, when your site visitors click on the slide image, a larger version of the image will be displayed in their browsers. Now you're ready to add the actual images to the slide show.

12 Click the value field next to imageURLs and then click Edit. When the Edit "imageURLs" Array dialog appears, click in the first field under Value and then click the folder icon. In the Select File dialog box, navigate to the lesson11 > images folder and select airplane.jpg; click OK (Windows) or Choose (MacOS). Click the second field and repeat this procedure to select snowboarder.jpg. Repeat the process a third time for the third field and select city.jpg. Click OK when you're done.

You're almost done! Next, let's add a title to the slide show.

13 In the title value field, enter **Reach for your goals** and press Tab.

The final task is to choose the slide transition. The default option, Random, applies any of the 10 available and changes with each slide. Let's choose a classic, but still classy approach instead.

14 From the transitionsType list, choose Fade.

💡 *If you simply want each slide to appear, choose None from the transitionsType list.*

Alright! Your slide show is now ready; let's see how it looks in the browser.

15 Choose File > Save and press F12 (Windows) or Option+F12 (MacOS) to preview the page in your primary browser. Click Play in the slide show viewer to begin the slide show. Note the accompanying captions that appear with each slide. Click on any slide to view the image in a larger format. When you're done, close your browser and return to Dreamweaver.

Congratulations, you've completed this lesson!

Review

▶ **Review questions**

1   True or False: Once you've inserted a Flash movie, there is no way to change whether the movie loops or not.

2   What are the two Flash video formats? Which does not require a specialized Web server?

3   After inserting a Flash element like the Image Viewer, how do you change the associated attributes?

▶ **Review answers**

1   False. You can change both the Loop and Autoplay attributes in the Property inspector.

2   Progressive download and streaming. Progressive download does not require a specialized server while streaming does.

3   Change attributes for Flash elements through the Flash elements panel, which appears whenever your instance of the Flash element is selected.

Time to share your well-crafted work with the world. For all the joy you receive by building an expertly designed Web site, nothing compares with viewing your work on the Web. But, before you can see your work online, you'll need to jump a few last hurdles, such as defining a remote site, checking your pages for cross-browser compatibility, validating your pages and putting them online. Get ready to take the final step!

12 | Publishing to the Web

In this lesson, you'll learn how to publish your Web site to the Internet and do the following:

- Define a remote site.
- Check pages for browser compatibility.
- Validate pages.
- Put files on the Web.
- Get pages from the Web.

This lesson will take about 90 minutes to complete. Be sure you have copied Lessons/Lesson12 from the Adobe Dreamweaver CS3 Classroom in a Book CD to your hard drive before beginning. As you work on this lesson, you'll overwrite the start files. If you need to restore the start files, copy them again from the CD.

Defining a remote site

Dreamweaver is based on a two site system. One site is set up on a folder on your computer and is known as a local site. All work in the previous lessons has taken place in your local site. The other site is established in a folder on a Web server on another computer: this is the remote site. The remote site is generally connected to the Internet and publicly available.

Dreamweaver provides a number of ways to connect to a remote site:

- FTP – Short for File Transfer Protocol, FTP is the standard method for connecting to hosted Web sites.

- Local/Network – A local or network connection is most frequently used when an intermediate Web server, called a staging server, is employed. Files from the staging server are then published to an Internet connected Web server.

- WebDav – The Web-based Distributed Authoring and Versioning or WebDav system is also known to Windows XP users as Web Folders.

- RDS –The Remote Development Services (RDS) was developed by Adobe (formerly Macromedia) for ColdFusion and is primarily used when working with ColdFusion-based sites.

- Microsoft Visual SourceSafe – A version control system that features check in/check out management and rollback capabilities.

The following exercises show you how to set up your remote site through the two most common methods: FTP and Local/Network.

Note: The following two exercises are mutually exclusive. If you have an Internet host and the details for establishing an FTP connection, follow the steps in "Setting up a remote FTP site." If you or your organization has access to their own Web server, follow the steps in "Establishing a remote site on a local or network server."

Setting up a remote FTP site

The vast majority of Web developers rely on FTP to publish and maintain their sites. A well-established protocol, there are many variations of FTP used on the Web, most of which are supported by Dreamweaver.

Note: You'll need access to a remote FTP server, including FTP address, username and password to complete this exercise.

1   Start Adobe Dreamweaver CS3.

2   If necessary, press F8 to open the Files panel and choose DW CIB from the site list.

3   Choose Site > Manage Sites.

4   When the Manage Sites dialog box appears, make sure that the current site, DW CIB is highlighted and click Edit.

💡 *To open the Site Definition for the current site directly, without opening the Manage Site dialog box, double-click the site name in the Files panel.*

5   In the Site Definition for DW CIB dialog box, make sure the Advanced tab is displayed and click Remote Info in the Category list.

6   From the Access list, choose FTP.

7   In the FTP host field, enter the Web address to your FTP server.

Typically, an FTP address looks like this: ftp.mySite.com. If you're unsure of your FTP address, contact your Web host.

8   In the Host directory field, enter the name of the folder that holds documents publicly accessible to the Web, if any.

Some Web hosts provide FTP access as a root level folder which might contain non-public folders—such as cgi-bin, used to store CGI (Common Gateway Interface) or binary scripts—as well as a publicly available folder. In these situations, enter the folder name—like public_html, wwwroot or www—in the Host directory field. With other Web hosts, the FTP address is the same as the public folder and the Host directory field should be left blank.

9 In the Login field, enter your FTP username and, in the Password field, enter your FTP password.

10 Click Test to verify that your FTP connection works properly.

11 Dreamweaver displays an alert to let you know whether the connection was successful or not; click OK to dismiss the alert.

12 If you don't want to reenter your username and password details every time Dreamweaver connects to your site, click Save.

13 Choose any options required for your FTP server:

• Use passive FTP – Allows your computer to make a necessary connection to the host computer and bypasses a firewall restraint; often used in conjunction with the Use firewall option.

• Use IPv6 transfer mode – Enables connection to IPv6-based servers, which utilize the most recent version of the Internet transfer protocol.

- Use firewall – Allows your computer to connect to the host computer from behind a firewall. Once this option is enabled, click Firewall Settings to define your firewall preferences such as port and firewall host.

- Use Secure FTP (SFTP) – Enables connection to hosts using SFTP.

14 If you still cannot connect to your FTP server, click Server Compatibility. Once the Server Compatibility dialog box opens, clear the Use FTP performance optimization option, click OK and click Test again.

15 Set any desired options for working with your remote site:

- Maintain synchronization information – Automatically notes which files have been changed on both the local and remote sites so they can be easily synchronized.

- Automatically upload files to server on save – Transfers files from the local to remote site when they are saved.

- Enable file check in and check out – Turns on the check in/check out system for collaborative website building with other team members. If you enable this option, you'll need to enter a user name for check out purposes and, optionally, an email address. If you're working by yourself, you do not need to enable file check in/check out.

16 Click OK when you're done. When the Manage Sites dialog box reappears, click Done.

Establishing a remote site on a local or network server

If your company or organization uses a staging server as a "middleman" between Web designers and the live Web site, it's likely you'll need to connect to your remote site on a local or network server. You can also use this type of connection on your own system, if it includes a Web server.

Note: You'll need access to a local or network Web server, including username and password to complete this exercise.

1   Start Adobe Dreamweaver CS3.

2   If necessary, press F8 to open the Files panel and choose DW CIB from the site list.

3   Choose Site > Manage Sites.

4   When the Manage Sites dialog box appears, make sure that the current site, DW CIB is highlighted and click Edit.

> 💡 *To open the Site Definition for the current site directly, without opening the Manage Site dialog box, double-click the site name in the Files panel.*

5   In the Site Definition for DW CIB dialog box, make sure the Advanced tab is displayed and click Remote Info in the Category list.

6   From the Access list, choose Local/Network.

If you're the Web server on your own system as a remote folder, point to the folder in your [system drive]:\Inetpub\wwwroot folder (Windows) or [system drive]:[username]: Sites folder (MacOS).

7   Set any desired options for working with your remote site:

•   Maintain synchronization information – Automatically notes which files have been changed on both the local and remote sites so they can be easily synchronized.

•   Automatically upload files to server on save – Transfers files from the local to remote site when they are saved.

•   Enable file check in and check out – Turns on the check in/check out system for collaborative website building with other team members. If you enable this option, you'll need to enter a user name for check out purposes and, optionally, an email address. If you're working by yourself, you do not need to enable file check in/check out.

8   Click OK when you're done. When the Manage Sites dialog box reappears, click Done.

Checking browser compatibility

Before pushing your site live to the Web, it's always a good idea to test it. To make sure your site is seen as intended, you'll need to verify that the pages are as compatible as possible with the browsers used by your target audience. The wide-spread use of CSS has introduced many issues, particularly with rendering the page, in various browsers. While many Web designers may have a number of the more recent browsers available to them—like Firefox, Internet Explorer, and Safari—most will not have access to all they need for complete testing. Luckily, a key feature of Dreamweaver CS3, Check Browser Compatibility, comes to the rescue.

Check Browser Compatibility combines in-product ease of use with online community support. When you run the Check Browser Compatibility feature, Dreamweaver inspects the current page and searches for any known CSS rendering issues. If a problem is found, it is listed in the Results panel along with a brief description. A link to the Adobe CSS Advisor is provided for a more complete explanation and one or more solutions or workarounds. The Adobe CSS Advisor, which can be found at www.adobe.com/go/cssadvisor, is a mini-site open to community experts who offer their expertise in CSS to identify browser issues and solutions.

In this exercise, you'll run the Check Browser Compatibility command to discover a CSS problem, identify the solution and fix the issue.

Note: This exercise requires a working connection to the Internet to be completed.

1   From the Files panel, expand the lesson12 folder and double-click the browsercheck_start.htm file to open it.

2   From the Check Page menu button (🖳) on the Document toolbar, choose Check Browser Compatibility.

3   In the Browser Check Compatibility category of the Results panel, review the description of the Expanding Box Problem. Note that the issue affects Internet Explorer 6.0 and is likely to occur.

The circular symbol at the start of each entry in the Browser Compatibility Check category indicates the likelihood of the problem being seen in browsers; a more a circle is filled with color, the more likely the code is to be an issue. The line number indicates the HTML element with the CSS style causing the problem.

Now that you've identified a problem, let's go find the solution.

Targeting your browsers

There are a great many browsers and browser versions in use around the world today. How does the Check Browser Compatibility feature know which browsers to check? The Target Browsers dialog box, accessible from the Settings menu option found under the Check Page menu button on the Document toolbar, lists six different browsers, in a range of versions:

- *Firefox, versions 1.0 – 2.0*

- *Internet Explorer, versions 5.0 – 7.0*

- *Internet Explorer for Macintosh, version 5.2*

- *Netscape, versions 7.0 – 8.0*

- *Opera, versions 7.0 – 9.0*

- *Safari, versions 1.0 – 2.0*

You can enable or disable each browser independently and set the minimum version to check. For example, if your browser stats showed that your site received a very low percentage of visitors who used Opera and Netscape 7.0 browsers, you could disable the Opera option completely and change the Netscape version to 8.0. Browser settings take place the next time you run Check Browser Compatibility.

4   Click the View solutions link. When the relevant page on the CSS Advisor site opens in your primary browser, read the Problem Solution and Detailed Description sections.

The solution offered that best fits the page—which includes both text and other content—is to apply an overflow: hidden CSS property to the containing elements. Let's go apply that solution now.

5   Close your browser and return to Dreamweaver. In the Browser Check Compatibility category of the Results panel, double-click the first problem entry.

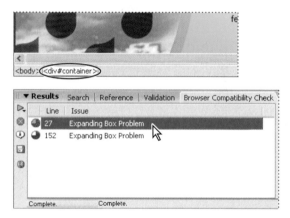

Note that the <div#container> element is highlighted in the Tag Selector.

6   Choose Window > CSS Styles. In the CSS Styles panel, click Current to switch to Current mode. In the Rules pane, choose the final entry, div#container.

Although you could choose Edit to open the CSS Rule Definition dialog box, let's add the needed property directly.

7   In the Properties pane of the CSS Styles panel, click Add Property. In the Property column, enter **overflow** and press Tab. From the list in the Value column, choose hidden.

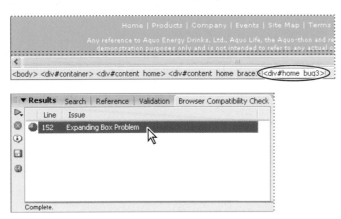

Let's continue and fix the second instance of the Expanding Box Problem.

8   In the Browser Check Compatibility category, click the green triangle (▷) and choose Check Browser Compatibility from the pop-up menu. Double-click the remaining entry in the Browser Check Compatibility category; note that the Tag Selector now shows <div#home_bug3>.

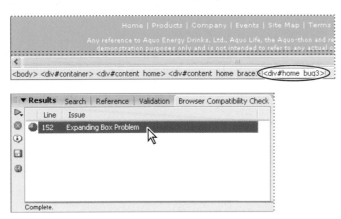

9   In the CSS Styles panel Rules pane, choose the final entry, div#home_bug3.

10   In the Properties pane of the CSS Styles panel, click Add Property. In the Property column, enter **overflow** and press Tab. From the list in the Value column, choose hidden.

11   Finally, let's verify that all the problems have been addressed.

12   In the Browser Check Compatibility category, click the green triangle (▷) and choose Check Browser Compatibility from the pop-up menu.

Congratulations, you've identified and corrected all the browser compatibility issues on this page: no CSS issues were found. You're one step closer to pushing it live.

13   Choose File > Save All.

In the next exercise, you'll make sure that you're working with valid code.

Validating your site

Although Dreamweaver writes valid HTML and XHTML throughout, it's always possible when hand-coding or combining elements to add invalid code to the page. Invalid code can lead to browser errors, so it's considered a best practice to always validate your site before publishing it to the Web. For your convenience, Dreamweaver provides a validation capability for checking an entire page, selected pages or the entire site.

1   If necessary, re-open the browsercheck_start.htm file worked on in the previous exercise by double-clicking its entry in the Files panel.

2   From the Validate Markup menu button (▷) on the Document toolbar, choose Validate Current Document.

In addition to validating the current document, you also have the option of validating the current site or validating files selected in the Files panel. Choose Settings to open the Validator category of Preferences and set the standard to validate against if there is no doctype tag.

3 When the Validation category of the Results panel opens, note the error presented. Select the error and, from the left side of the Results panel, click More Info (ⓘ).

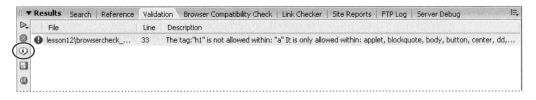

Dreamweaver has found a problem with the code where an <a> is wrapped around an <h1> tag instead of being within it.

4 Review the information in the Description dialog box; when you're done, click OK.

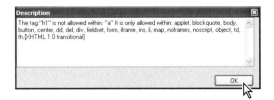

5 Double-click the error in the Validation category to go to the problematic code in Code view.

To resolve this problem, you'll need to reposition the <h1> tag pair so that they wrap around the <a> tag pair.

6 Drag the selected <h1> tag in front of the <a> tag on the same line. Select the closing </h1> tag after the text Aquo and drag it after the closing </a>. When you're done, click Design.

Now let's make sure that error is gone for good!

7   In the Validation category, click the green triangle and choose Validate Current Document from the pop-up menu.

Your Web page now has a clean bill of health and is ready to be published.

8   Choose File > Save.

Putting your site online

For the most part, the local site and the remote site are mirror-images of each other and contain the same HTML files, images and other assets in the same folder structure. When you transfer a Web page from your local site to your remote site, you are publishing or putting that page. If you put a file stored within a folder in your local site, Dreamweaver transfers the file to the equivalent folder; it will even automatically create the folder on the remote site if necessary.

With Dreamweaver, you can publish anything from a single file to a complete site in a single operation. When you publish a Web page, Dreamweaver asks if you would like to put the dependent files as well. Dependent files are the images, Flash movies, JavaScript files, CSS external style sheets, server side includes and any other file that is necessary to complete the page. Dreamweaver automatically puts all of your dependent files in the proper folders to match their locations on your local site.

Note: This exercise assumes you have established a remote site, either with an FTP or local/network connection as described in "Defining a remote site" section of this lesson.

1   If necessary, re-open the browsercheck_start.htm file worked on in the previous exercise by double-clicking its entry in the Files panel.

2 From the File Management menu button (▒) on the Document toolbar, choose Put.

💡 *Dreamweaver provides a great many ways to put files online. You can choose Site > Put for the current page or select the file in the Files panel and choose Put, the Up arrow icon. The Files panel is also great for transferring multiple files—just select what you want to transfer, whether individual files or complete folders—and click Put.*

3 When the Dependent Files dialog appears, click Yes.

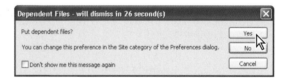

When might you not want to put your dependent files? Generally, only when you're making a change to a file already on the Web. If you've just made a change to the code on the page and not altered any of the associated images or other attached assets, there's no need to put your dependent files again.

4 If necessary, choose Window > Files to display the Files panel. Click Expand/Collapse (▒), the last icon on the right of the Files panel.

A single Web page, even with a number of dependent files, is likely to be published so quickly you won't have a chance to see Dreamweaver's Background File Activity dialog box. Dreamweaver transfers files as a separate computer process, so if there are lengthy uploads, you can continue working in Dreamweaver while the files are being published.

When the file transfer is complete, it's time to go see how Dreamweaver did.

5   When the Site window is expanded, click Connect (🦮) to connect to your remote site. When the folders are displayed, expand the lesson12 folder to review the transferred files.

The HTML file, browser_start.htm, and all the dependent files have been successfully transferred, with the same folder structure as on the local site.

Note: The opposite of Put is Get; you can get any file from the remote site by selecting it in the Remote pane and clicking Get, the down arrow. Alternatively, you can simply drag the file from one pane to the other. It is important to note that any files transferred from your remote site to local site (or vice-versa) automatically overwrite the equivalent file.

6   Expand any folders on the remote site to confirm that the files were transferred successfully. When you're done exploring, click Connect to break the connection and Expand/Collapse to return to the Document window in Dreamweaver.

Congratulations, you've completed this lesson!

Review

▶ **Review questions**

1 What is a remote site?

2 Name two types of file transfer supported in Dreamweaver.

3 True or False: Once the Check Browser Compatibility feature has located a CSS problem, you have to provide the solution yourself.

4 Is it possible to validate your Web pages from within Dreamweaver? If so, how?

5 True or False: You have to publish every file and associated image, JavaScript file or server-side include manually.

▶ **Review answers**

1 A remote site is a mirror image of your local site; the remote site is stored on a Web server connected to the Internet.

2 FTP (File Transfer Protocol) and Local/Network are the two most commonly used. Other file transfer possibilities in Dreamweaver include WebDav, Visual SourceSafe and RDS.

3 False. The results of the Check Browser Compatibility operation connect to the CSS Advisor which contains full descriptions of the problem and available solutions.

4 Yes, you can validate your Web pages from within Dreamweaver by choosing any of the options from the Validate Markup menu button such as Validate Current Page.

5 False. Dreamweaver will automatically transfer dependent files, including embedded or referenced images, CSS style sheets and Flash movies.

Index

Symbols

<body> tags 146
<div> tags 150, 156
    nesting 156
    styled 163
<form> tags 232, 233

A

Accessibility preferences 236
accessible forms 236
Access key field, forms 238
Accordion, Spry
    incorporating 216
    showing and hiding page content
      216
actions
    editing 179
    triggering behaviors 177
active content
    with Internet Explorer 268
Adobe Bridge 126
Adobe CSS Advisor
    identifying CSS rendering
      problems 292
Adobe Design Center 3
Adobe Dreamweaver CS3
    installing 2
Adobe Fireworks 117
Adobe Flash. *See* Flash movies
Adobe Photoshop CS3 Classroom in
  a Book
    CD contents ix
Adobe Training and Certification
  programs 4
Ajax (Asynchronous JavaScript and
  XML) 201
All mode 15
Allow Blocked Content, Internet
  Explorer 230
alt text 107
anchor links 134
AP elements 192
Assets panel
    adding images 107
Attach Style Sheet command 63
Autoplay attributes, changing 270

B

background color 148
Background File Activity dialog box
  300
background images
    inserting 17, 110
banner, adding 160
behaviors 177
    editing 189
    multiple 180
    Open Browser Window 187
    Swap Image 182
    triggers 183
Behaviors panel 179
body tag
    defining 146
Bridge CS3 126
    browse from Dreamweaver 126
    place in Dreamweaver 127
Brightness and Contrast tool, images
  117
Browse for File
    setting links 135
Browse for Folder
    setting internal links 135
Browse in Bridge command 127
browsers
    compatibility 292
    reviewing pages in 22
    selecting 294
bulleted lists 90
buttons
    moving label text 256
    radio 247
    submit 256

C

captions
    linking to images in slide shows
      278
Cascading Style Sheets. *See* CSS
  entries; *See* style sheets, cascading
CDATA delimiter 206
checkboxes 250
Check Browser Compatibility
  command 292

chrome 151, 188
classes, custom 69
Classroom in a Book files
    copying 2
Code preferences 268
Code view 32
ColdFusion
    connecting to a remote server
      286
Collapsible Panel, Spry 216
color, background 148
color, text
    changing 19
color scheme
    slide show 276
columns
    changing number of 78
    setting in page layout 161
Compact mode, Bridge 128
Crop tool, images 117
CSS classes
    styling data with 211
CSS layouts 146
CSS properties 67
    Background category 110
    Block category 70
    Box category 67
    changing 72
    List category 92
    Type category 66, 77
CSS rendering problems
    identifying 292
CSS Rule Definition for #content
  dialog box 154
CSS Rule Definition for #header
  dialog box 153
CSS Rule Definition for #leftColumn
  dialog box 162
CSS Rule Definition for #wrapper
  dialog box 150
CSS Rule Definition for Body dialog
  box 148
CSS rules 65
    changing list format 91
    editing 159
    for page layout 146
    for tables 259
    inserting background images 110

CSS styles
  adding 219
  applying 71
  attaching 63
  exporting 168
  modifying 73
CSS Styles panel 15, 41, 148
Current mode 15
custom classes 69

D

data, tabular
  importing 100
data sets, Spry
  building 210
data types
  changing 207
Design view 32
detail regions, nested 216
detail regions, Spry
  applying 213
  identifying 214
Document toolbar 33, 49
document window 32
Dreamweaver behaviors 177
Dreamweaver CS3
  installing 2
drop-down lists 253
dummy links, in behaviors 177
dynamic images
  adding 213
  associating 219
dynamic text elements
  adding 213

E

Edit Photoshop command 126
Edit tool, images 116
email links 138
error messages
  editing 241, 243
Export dialog box 118
Export Slices command 118
external style sheets 62
eyedropper tool 78

F

favorites 53
fields, password 244

fieldset
  grouping form elements 257
File Transfer Protocol (FTP). *See also* FTP entries
  connecting to a remote site 285
Fireworks 117
Flash elements
  for slide shows 274
Flash Media Server 271
Flash movies 266
  adding 267
  previewing 270
Flash Player 267
Flash slide shows 274
Flash videos 266, 271
  previewing 273
  progressive download 271
  streaming 271
Flexible Marketing Area (FMA) 269
float property 78
  setting columns 162
fonts, changing 19
Form objects
  accessibility 236
  buttons 256
  checkboxes 250
  lists 253
  password text field 244
  radio buttons 247
  Spry text field 239
  text area 245
  text field 236
forms 229
  about 232
  accessible 236
  Access key field 238
  adding text fields 235
  adding to pages 233
  framing 257
  Tab Index 238
frameColor color swatch 276
frameShow 277
FTP site, remote
  setting up 286

G

global settings 150
graphic links, internal 134
graphics, sliced 118
graphic tools 116
gripper 44

guides
  displaying measurements with 171
  viewing 170

H

headings
  creating 85
  editing 10
  formatting with Property inspector 85
help
  Dreamweaver 3
highlighting
  with Spry Effects 204, 222
HTML and Images option 118

I

imageCaptions 277
image format, changing 114
Image icon 107
imageLinks 277
Image placeholders 165
image placeholders 109
Image Preview dialog box 114, 124, 125
images
  adding with Assets panel 107
  background 110
  editing 116
  inserting 12, 106
  inserting background 17
  in Web pages 105
  linking captions in slide show 278
  optimizing 111
  resizing 113
  tiling 111
images, dynamic
  adding 213
  associating 219
Image Viewer 274
  resizing 275
Insert Fireworks HTML dialog box 120
Insert Other Character dialog box 140
Insert Spry Table dialog box 210
Insert Text dialog box 88

Insert toolbar 49
adding <div> tags 156
Flash 269
images 107
Photoshop files 112
placeholders 109
rollovers 120
setting email links 138
setting page layout 152
internal site links 134
Internet Explorer
issues with active content 268

J

JavaScript
in Spry effects 222
in Spry Text fields 240

L

layouts, page
columns 161
CSS-based 145
layouts, site
importing from Photoshop 124
legend
grouping form elements 257
links 133
anchor 134
creating 14
dummy, in behaviors 177
email 138
external 137
internal 134
showing and hiding 75
targeted 139
lists
drop-down 253
editing with CSS rules 91
numbered 90
List Values dialog box 255
local or network connection
connecting to a remote site 285, 291
local site 59, 285
logo, adding 157
Loop attributes, editing 270

M

magnification, changing 36
Manage Sites dialog box 287, 291

margins 149
Menu Bar, Spry 216
Microsoft Visual SourceSafe
connecting to a remote server 286
Move CSS Styles command 168
movies. *See* Flash movies
multimedia, incorporating 265
MySpace command 45

N

Named Anchor dialog box 141
navigation elements
showing and hiding 75
nested detail regions 216
New CSS Rule command 66, 69, 75, 148, 150
New Document dialog box 8, 147
new page, creating 8
New Site command 60
no-repeat option 111
numbered lists 90

O

online help. *See* help
Open Browser Window behavior 187
Open Browser Window dialog box 179
Open icon 30
Optimize, images 113, 116
options
checkboxes 250
mutually exclusive 247

P

padding 149
page areas
defining 152
moving 79
showing and hiding 75, 192
page layouts
columns 161
CSS-based 145
Page Properties dialog box 48
pages. *See also* Web pages
pages, interactive 177
pages, new 8
pages, recent
opening 30

page title
editing 10
page width
setting 150
panels
managing 38
rearranging 39
regrouping 42
resizing 41
showing and hiding 44
password fields 244
Photoshop files
inserting 121
Photoshop images
copying and pasting 124
Photoshop layouts
importing 124
placeholders
forms 233
image 109
inserting 165
Point to File option
setting links 136
pop-up windows 187
preferences
accessibility 236
code 268
customizing 54
setting 3
validator 298
Preview in Browser command 23
previewing
Flash movies 270
Flash videos 273
progressive download
Flash videos 271
properties, CSS 67
Property inspector 13, 46
behaviors 183
creating external links 137
creating internal links 135
email addresses 241
forms 233
heading formatting 85
pop-up windows 188
previewing Flash movies 270
setting links 141
table formatting, Spry 212
PSD files, inserting 121

Q

Quick Tag Editor 215

R

radio buttons 247
  accessibility 249
Radio Group dialog box 247
RDS
  connecting to a remote server
    286
recent pages
  opening 30
Refresh Design View command 34
regions, Spry
  updating 211
regions, Spry detail
  applying 213
  identifying 214
remote FTP site
  setting up 286
remote site 59, 285
Resample tool, images 117
rollovers 117, 182
rulers 170
rules, CSS 65
  editing 72

S

Save Web Image dialog box 123, 125
Save Workspace Layout dialog box
  45
searching and replacing 94
Select Image Source dialog box 13,
  107
server, staging 285
Set Magnification menu 37
settings, global 150
Sharpen tool, images 117
showing and hiding page areas 192
showing and hiding page content
  with Spry Accordion 216
sites
  defining 59
  local and remote 285
  putting online 299
  validating 297
size, text
  changing 21
skin, for video controls 272
slices, exporting 118
slide shows. *See also* Flash slide shows
  adding titles 279
slide transitions 280

spacing, text
  changing 21
spell checking 92
Split view 32, 33
Spry 203
Spry Accordion panel 216, 217
Spry Assets folder 208
Spry Collapsible Panel 216
Spry Data
  working with XML schema 206
Spry data sets
  building 210
Spry Data types
  about 208
Spry detail regions
  applying 213
  identifying 214
Spry effects 204, 222
Spry Form widgets 230
Spry Menu Bar 216
Spry regions
  updating 211
Spry Tabbed Panels 216
Spry Table 210
  adding 210
Spry Text fields 235, 239, 242
Spry Validation Text Field object
  239, 242
Spry Widgets
  constructing 216
  form 230
Spry XML Data Set dialog box 207
staging server 285
Standard toolbar 50
starting points 8
Status bar 35
streaming Flash video 271
style
  applying 70
Style Rendering toolbar 50, 74
style sheets
  attaching 63
style sheets, cascading 59
  editing 15
  editing for print 73, 77
  editing styles 72
  inserting background images 110
style sheets, external 62
  85
submit button 256
Swap Image behavior
  for rollovers 182

T

Tabbed Panels, Spry 216
Tab Index
  forms 238
tables
  creating 96
  CSS styling 259
  holding forms 234
tabular data
  importing 100
tags
  defining styles for 65
tags, <body> 146
tags, <div> 150, 156
  nesting 156
  styled 163
tags, <form> 232, 233
Tag Selector 35
  applying CSS styles 71
Target Browsers dialog box 294
targeted links 139
text
  changing font and color 19
  changing size and spacing 21
  editing 11
  formatting 86
  importing 87
  searching and replacing 94
  working with 83
text areas 245
text elements, dynamic
  adding 213
text fields
  adding to forms 235
text form elements
  adding 235
text links
  internal 134
titles
  adding to slide shows 279
toolbars 49
  Document 33
  Insert 49, 107, 109, 112, 120, 138,
    152, 156, 269
  Standard 50
  Style Rendering 50, 74
training and certification programs 4
transitions, slide 280
triggers 182

U

user guide 3

V

validating sites 297
validation 230
 form fields 239
 forms 241
 triggering 241
Validator preferences 298
videos. *See* Flash videos

W

WebDav
 connecting to a remote server
 286
Web pages. *See also* page entries
 reviewing in browsers 22
web pages
 validating 297
Welcome screen 29
windows, pop-up 187
Word documents
 importing 88
workspace
 customizing 29
 restoring 45
 saving custom 45
wrapper 150

X

XML data source
 establishing 205
XML schema
 Spry Data object 206

Z

Zoom tool 36

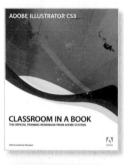

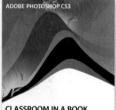